MONTANA WILDLANDS
FROM NORTHWEST PEAKS TO DEADHORSE BADLANDS

BY BILL CUNNINGHAM

MONTANA GEOGRAPHIC SERIES
NUMBER 16

MONTANA MAGAZINE
AMERICAN GEOGRAPHIC PUBLISHING
HELENA, MONTANA

To all those who have taken pen or microphone in hand in defense of Montana's wild places; and especially to the late Senator Lee Metcalf, to Lee's quiet man behind the scenes, Teddy Roe, and to Donna Metcalf, who inspires us with her continued dedication to her husband's legacy and, in so doing, has created a legacy of her own.

ISBN 0-938314-93-9

Text © 1990 Bill Cunningham
© 1990 American Geographic
  Publishing
P.O. Box 5630, Helena, MT 59604
(406) 443-2842

William A. Cordingley, Chairman
Rick Graetz, President & CEO
Mark O. Thompson, Director of
  Publications
Barbara Fifer, Production Manager
Design by Linda Collins
Photo editing by John Reddy
Printed in Korea by Dong-A
  Printing through Códra
  Enterprises, Torrance, CA

American Geographic Publishing is a corporation for publishing illustrated geographic information and guides. It is not associated with American Geographical Society. It has no commercial or legal relationship to and should not be confused with any other company, society or group using the words geographic or geographical in its name or its publications.

PAT O'HARA

ACKNOWLEDGMENTS

This book, although broadly descriptive in nature, is nonetheless a composite of decades of wandering within, thinking about, and fighting for wildlands throughout Montana. With that many years, it is difficult to pinpoint my indebtedness to so many people. I am certainly grateful to all those who supplied information about areas and issues portrayed in the following pages. More than anything, I want to thank those who helped shape my personal wildland philosophy when, as a young forester, I could just as easily have taken the utilitarian road of sawlog forestry. Mentors and teachers who deserve special thanks include Arnold Bolle, Doris Milner, G.M. Brandborg, Bill Bishop, Stewart Brandborg, Jim Posewitz, Liz Smith, Cecil Garland, Don Aldrich, and Clif Merritt. There are others, but please know that you are not forgotten.

ABOUT THE AUTHOR

Bill Cunningham vigorously pursues his life-long love affair with Montana wildlands with a blend of writing, photography, back-country teaching and outfitting. As former Montana field representative for The Wilderness Society and conservation director of the Montana Wilderness Association, he was involved in the political process that designated many of the Wilderness areas in Montana. He lives on a family ranch near Missoula and is the author of *Montana's Continental Divide* in the Montana Geographic Series, as well as the wildlands column in *Montana Magazine*.

JOHN REDDY

MICHAEL S. QUINTON

JOHN REDDY

Above: *Contest of the monarchs.*
Left: *Tongue River badlands.*

Facing page: *Lower Aero Lake Area, Absaroka-Beartooth Wilderness.*
Title page: *Snowcrest Mountains moonrise.* JOHN REDDY

Front cover: *Sky Top Lakes Basin, Gallatin National Forest in the Absaroka-Beartooth Wilderness.* PAT O'HARA
Back cover, top left: *Peregrine falcon.* TOM J. ULRICH
Top right: *Looking east from the Pryor Mountains to Bighorn Canyon and the Bighorn Mountains.* GEORGE WUERTHNER
Bottom: *The Continental Divide from Prairie Reef in the Bob Marshall Wilderness Area.* PAT O'HARA

PREFACE

Realities of space, time and energy do wonders to narrow down the scope of overly ambitious endeavors. Such is the case with this portrait of Montana's many and varied wildlands. When I embarked upon this project I had grandiose visions of writing a far more definitive work. The complete political, administrative and natural history of every major wildland in the state would be presented. Even lesser areas would be described in depth. Or so I thought. I owe publishers Rick Graetz and Mark Thompson a debt of gratitude for making me realize that an "encyclopaedia of wildlands" is not only beyond the scope of the Montana Geographic Series but beyond the interest of most people.

I hope the following pages embody a more manageable and interesting look at wildlands across Montana, along with major management issues that influence their future. The idea is to give readers a solid geographic point of reference for what continues to be one of Montana's major land uses: wildness.

I'll admit that the broader initial design for this work stemmed from my many years of activism in the ongoing saga of Montana wilderness politics. I've long known that I could never write a book on the subject as long as I was consumed by in day-to-day conservation issues. Having been retired from the front lines of wilderness battles for more than five years, I feel seasoned enough to assume a broader, more detached view, but with enough emotional involvement to capture a bit of what is so special about our remaining vestiges of wild country.

Wilderness is my life and its relative abundance here is why I choose to live and work in Montana. I hope that this book will give you a taste of what lies beyond the end of the road. May these images and narratives motivate you to explore, cherish and defend these last best places, whether you choose to do so on the land or vicariously, with the reassurance that we still have country worthy of the name, "Montana Wildlands."

JOHN REDDY

RONALD J. GLOVAN

Above: Mt. Evans in the Anaconda Range and subalpine larch in autumn dress.
Left: Bitterroot blossom.

Facing page: Dawn breaks over the Lolo National Forest.

CHARLES E. KAY

CONTENTS

Acknowledgments 3
Preface 4
Introduction 6
Montana Wildlands map .... follows 8
The Cabinet-Yaak 12
**Greater Glacier/
  Bob Marshall Country** 20
The Upper Clark Fork 40
Northern Bitterroot Divide 48
Upper Missouri/Great Divide 56
Greater Yellowstone 68
Wild Islands in the Prairie 80
Wildlands of the Lower Missouri .. 90
**Wildlands of the
  Lower Yellowstone** 98
For Further Information 103
Epilogue 104

INTRODUCTION

By any measure Montana is richly endowed with wild country, so much so that wildness is woven into its identity as a place and as a state of mind. The following pages portray a wild heritage unsurpassed in the continental United States—nearly 12.4 million acres in 89 wildlands or clusters of wildlands totaling 197 individual contiguous roadless areas. On one level this incredible number and diversity of natural landscapes is at once our pride in the present and our geography of hope. On another level comes the sobering thought that, a scant 150 years ago, all of what we now call Montana was a single vast wilderness surrounded by still more expanses of wild country in every direction. Montana has changed from one 93-million-acre roadless area to hundreds of wild remnants averaging just under 63,000 acres each, separated by more than 80 million acres of cities, towns, highways, agricultural land, mines and clearcuts.

As vast as it is, wildland no longer dominates our vistas and horizons. Only two dozen undeveloped enclaves exceed 100,000 acres in size and of these, only the Bob Marshall Country and the Absaroka-Beartooth complex encompass more than the magic figure of 1 million untrammeled acres. The second-largest area is only half the size of the largest, and the third in size is less than half as big as the second. Our progressive chipping away at wild spaces has been profound, with an unknown loss of genetic diversity as the distance shrinks from perimeter to core.

Still, the extent of Montana wildlands is extraordinary, and is more of a cause for celebration than chagrin. Despite our heavy hand upon the land, natural processes prevail from lofty peaks to sweeping prairies.

A chapter is devoted to each of nine distinct physiographic regions, from the lush Cabinet-Yaak to the dry Lower Yellowstone. Wherever possible, the regions are drawn on the basis of topography, but mostly they differ by the nature of the land within their approximate borders. All of the wildlands described within each region possess similar landforms, climate, vegetation and wildlife.

Based on the criteria of proximity, similarity and contiguity, Montana's wild places logically fit within 89 separate roadless areas or complexes of areas. An example of a wildland complex is the Eastern Little Belts, where 11 neighboring roadless areas share common natural attributes. Single areas range from the 2½-million-acre Bob Marshall Country to the Square Butte Natural Area of fewer than 2,000 acres. The guiding principle is contiguity. The most frequent abuse of roadless resources is fragmentation, where arbitrary political boundaries artificially reduce their significance as wilderness. Hence the emphasis on keeping wildlands whole. For example, instead of considering the Sapphires apart from the Anaconda-Pintler Wilderness, the country is viewed here as part of a single contiguous wildland of nearly 368,000 acres.

Scotchman Peaks and the Rocky Mountain Front are among the very few wildlands that exist as complete landforms. In most cases wildness is synonymous with roadlessness which, by definition, begins where development leaves off—often midslope and without regard to topography and other natural features.

Acreages presented are the most accurate estimates possible of the total wildland within each area, irrespective of land ownership. Most of this undisturbed land is federal, with national forest being the overwhelming component. However, substantial inholdings, peripheral lands and, in some cases, entire areas are private, state or tribal. National forest acreages are based on the 1983 forest plan revisions except where intervening development caused reductions. In a few instances, adjacent unroaded state and private lands expand the boundary beyond the Forest Service inventory. Each area has at least 5,000 contiguous acres within Montana, or by its nature can be preserved, as with islands or isolated prairie buttes. Aside from ownership, all of the areas described in the succeeding chapters meet the minimum requirements of the Wilderness Act. The act provides a solid point of reference, but no suggestion is made that Wilderness designation is the best form of management for every wildland. I invite you to explore these mostly unknown places and make your own judgment.

Describing these 12.4 million roadless acres offers but a snapshot in time in the continuing drama between preservation and development. Only about 29 out of every 100 wild acres are in the National Wilderness System, with much of the remainder either in some lesser protective status, or else too high, rocky, steep or remote to encourage development. Still, about half of Montana's wild country lacks legal or physical protection. Congress has many powers but it cannot create wilderness. With enough persuasion from the people it can *protect* some of our wildland legacy, but we will never again have as much wilderness as existed at the time the "snapshot" of this book was taken.

JOHN REDDY

Above: *Small Creek, Anaconda-Pintler Wilderness.*
Facing page: *The McDonald Creek Valley, Glacier National Park* JEFF GNASS

DIANE ENSIGN

Above: Packing hunters' supplies into the Bob Marshall Wilderness.
Right: Along Belt Creek in the Little Belt Mountains.

JOHN REDDY

Wilderness proposals range from the militant stance of Earth First! who can see no good reason why a single wild acre should be lost to the "no more Wilderness" posture of the "Wise Use" movement. In between are the positions of the governor of Montana, the Montana Wildlands Coalition, millworkers and conservationists, the Forest Service, the timber industry and members of the Montana congressional delegation. Ultimately, each of these positions is politically motivated and arbitrary, in that boundaries are drawn and areas omitted, taking in or leaving out suitable or unsuitable land for Wilderness, depending upon one's point of view. (Throughout this book capitalized Wilderness refers to a formally-designated Wilderness Area.)

Although I readily admit a clear, unabashed bias for Wilderness, an assessment of each major state-wide proposal, and of its underlying politics, is a book in its own right that needs to be written. But here an effort is made to describe what remains of wild Montana and not how the politicians and interest groups would slice it up to appease their constituencies. It has not been easy to write about Montana wildlands during an election year when chaos and confusion clouded the debate over the long-elusive Montana Wilderness Bill. Beyond the vagaries of short-term expediency and political compromise there emerges an astounding reality—wild country that you can likely see on the horizon from your Montana home or neighborhood.

If wilderness is timeless, than its preservation is truly our society's ultimate act of humility. We encase these lands in a living museum called the Wilderness System, not so much for ourselves, but from ourselves, for the benefit of generations yet unborn. We take pride in deliberately slowing our headlong rush to drill the last barrel, cut the last ancient tree, harness the last wild river. To the wilderness hunter, the kill comes hard, rather than easy. The back-country angler revels in the setting and in the rhythm of wind and water. Mules and misery whips replace pickups and chain saws and, in so doing, allow us to find something in ourselves we thought lost.

The freedom of wilderness brings stability, a feeling of reality and certainty to a shaky world. Here we find the real Montana—where perpetual wildness flows through both the land and a people close to the land.

Cascade patterns on a summer afternoon in Glacier National Park. JEFF GNASS

WILDLANDS MAP FOLDOUT

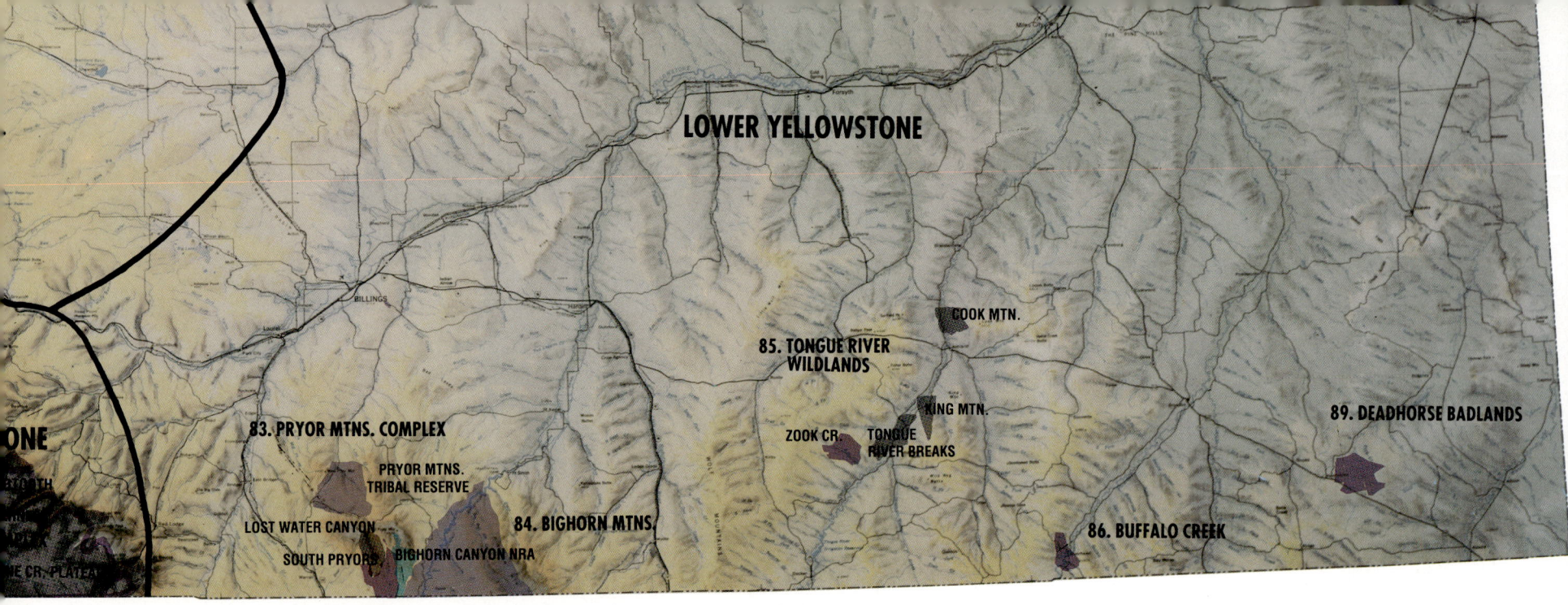

MONTANA WILDLANDS AND WILDERNESS AREAS

I. Cabinet/Yaak
Total Wildlands: 532,252 acres. Wilderness: 94,272 acres (17.8%)

II. Glacier/Bob Marshall
Total Wildlands: 3,958,310 acres. Wilderness: 1,698,729 acres (42.9%)

III. Upper Clark Fork
Total Wildlands: 779,803 acres. Wilderness: 60,979 acres (7.8%)

IV. Northern Bitterroot Divide
Total Wildlands: 910,847 acres. Wilderness: 251,343 acres (27.7%)

V. Upper Missouri/Great Divide
Total Wildlands: 1,651,300 acres. Wilderness: 157,874 acres (9.6%)

VI. Greater Yellowstone
Total Wildlands: 2,474,679 acres. Wilderness: 1,207,604 acres (49.0%)

VII. Wild Islands in the Prairie
Total Wildlands: 1,249,214 acres. Wilderness: 28,562 acres (2.3%)

VIII. Lower Missouri
Total Wildlands: 545,302 acres. Wilderness: 32,185 acres (5.9%)

IX. Lower Yellowstone
Total Wildlands: 378,635 acres. Wilderness: 0 acres

Statewide Total of **Wildlands**: 12,399,757 acres
Designated **Wilderness**: 3,531,548 acres (16 areas/28.5%)

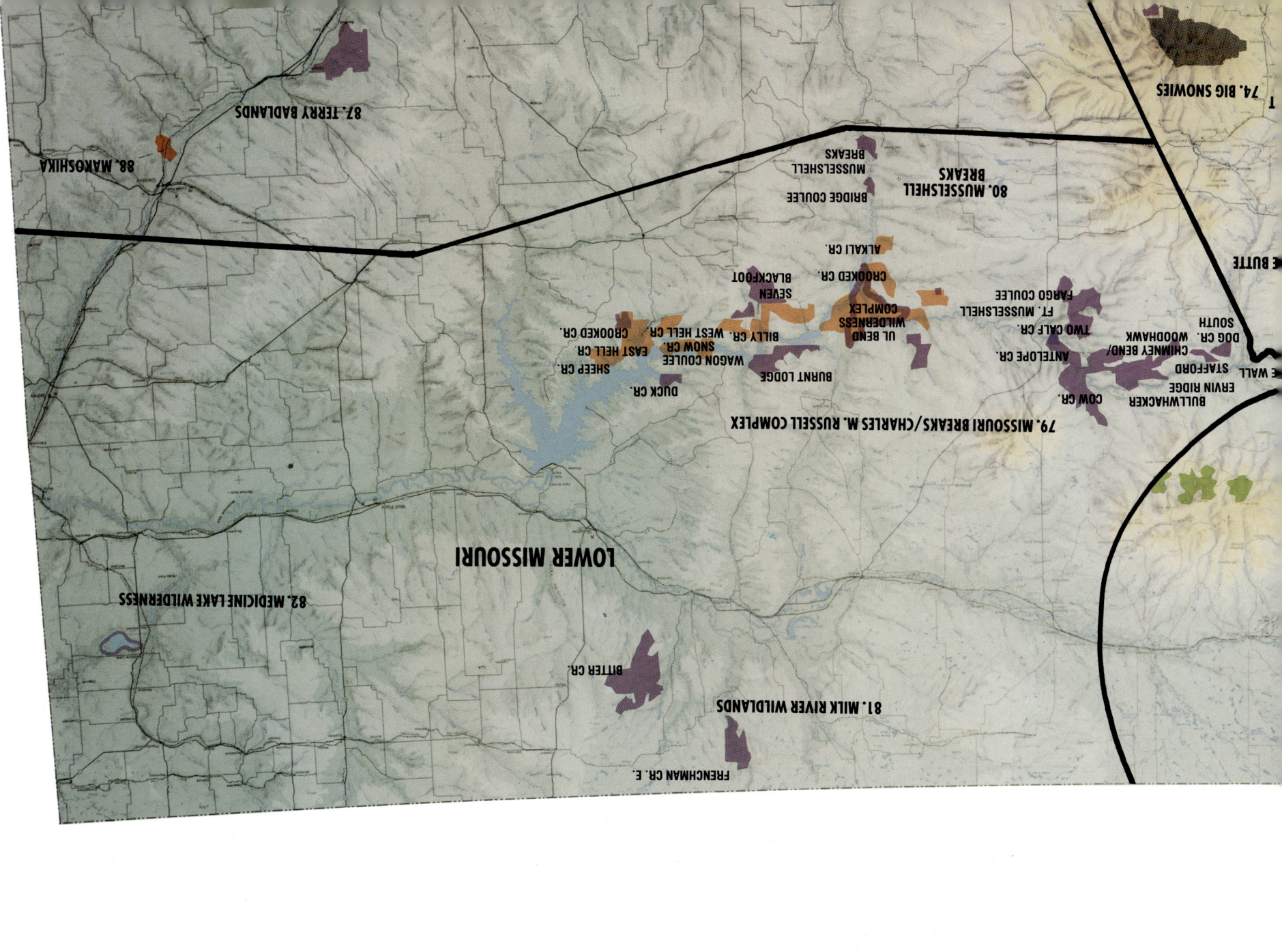

LANDMARK ACCORDS FOR KOOTENAI AND LOLO NATIONAL FORESTS

News reports of angry Montana woods workers at noisy anti-wilderness rallies encircled by log trucks with blaring air horns have been common in recent years. These images reinforce the notion that the gap never will be bridged between the preservers and developers of our remaining wild forests. A dramatic turnaround came during spring 1990, when local mill workers, sportsmen and conservationists decided to talk with, instead of about, each other face to face concerning specific roadless areas and issues on the timber-dominated Kootenai and Lolo national forests of northwest Montana. Together these two forests contribute 62 percent of the state's annual national forest timber harvest. After four months of negotiations, the parties signed separate agreements for each forest, which divided unprotected roadless areas into two categories: recommended Wilderness and lands that would be released to nonwilderness uses, such as timbering. Absent is the traditional "study" category because the negotiators, unlike some politicians, had no arbitrary upper limit on wilderness acreage.

In the words of Jim Cullen, president of the local lumber and industrial union that represents workers at the W.I. Forest Products mill in Thompson Falls, "We were tired of reading press releases designed to fan the flames and block any constructive solutions." By talking "...with people who wanted to resolve the wilderness issue...we discovered that if you take away the sources of inflammation, the wound can heal." As a result, in June 1990 the accords were signed by representatives of seven local AFL-CIO mill worker unions, the Montana Wilderness Association, Montana Wildlands Coalition, Kootenai Wildlands Alliance, Montana Outfitters & Guides Association, Libby Rod & Gun Club, Kootenai Fly Fishers, Backcountry Horsemen, Western Montana Fish & Game Association, concerned Citizens of Superior Ranger District, and the Great Burn Study Group.

In general, the accords embodied the conservationist "Alternative W" wilderness proposal for the two forests while making available for logging roughly 98 percent of the "suitable timber land" identified in the two forest plans. Still, not all conservationists embraced the accords. The Missoula-based Alliance for the Wild Rockies is advocating a broader bioregional approach. The Alliance has raised important questions about wildlife needs, old growth and bio-diversity on the more than 400,000 Lolo Forest roadless acres that would be removed from wilderness consideration if the accord becomes law.

Although the accords focused mainly on timber, they have shaken twin pillars of anti-wilderness arguments by overcoming the "wilderness versus jobs" issue and the claim that wilderness is supported mostly by "outsiders." As Jim Cullen said, "when local people put their heads together, miracles can happen." Indeed, the new trust and dialogue established between traditional adversaries bodes will for improved management and protection of Montana's wildlands.

Lolo National Forest Accord

The following areas would be designated Wilderness under the terms of this agreement:

Area	Total Acreage
Cube Iron/Mt. Silcox	37,700
Great Burn	92,700
Sheep Mountain	28,000
Quigg Peak	60,100
Monture Creek Addition	68,600
Portions of these areas are on the Lolo National Forest:	
Swan Front (Bob Marshall Wilderness)	9,000
Stony Mountain	31,000
Lolo Peak (Selway-Bitterroot Wilderness)	3,700
(Selway-Bitterroot Wilderness)	
Cataract Peak (mostly Kootenai Natl. Forest)	7,000
Total Wilderness	**337,800**
Total Roadless Lands	
Released for Non-Wilderness Use	400,400

Kootenai National Forest (KNF) Accord

The following areas would be designated Wilderness under the terms of the agreement:

Area	Total Acreage
Cabinet Mountains Wilderness Additions	86,800
Scotchman Peaks	54,280
Galena	19,300
Cataract Creek	17,900
Cube Iron (mostly Lolo National Forest)	400
Trout Creek	28,000
Ten Lakes	44,500
Buckhorn Ridge	22,600
Thompson-Seton (also Flathead Natl. For.)	20,000 (KNF)
Tuchuck (also Flathead Natl. Forest)	2,300 (KNF)
Roderick Mountain	22,900
Grizzly Peak	4,500
Northwest Peak Scenic Area	20,330
Total Wilderness	**343,810**
Total Roadless Lands	
Released for Non-Wilderness Use	94,490

WILDLANDS EDUCATION: ON THE LAND WHERE IT COUNTS

BILL CUNNINGHAM PHOTOS

Above: Kari Gunderson, wildlands educator, on the North Fork, Birch Creek.
Right: Coach and students on the Dearborn River, Rocky Mountain Front.

Since 1984, the Mission Mountains have been the nation's first and only Wilderness where actual on-the-ground stewardship of the land is taken over not by Forest Service employees, but by private contractors. Kari Gunderson and Joe Flood, partners both in marriage and in wilderness management, are driven not by the modest dollar amount of their contract but by that special quality of dedication that cannot be purchased by any sum of money.

As wilderness rangers, their activities include opening 45 miles of trails, doing back-country cleanup, collecting data for the Limits of Acceptable Change process, "naturalizing" abused and overused campsites, and meeting visitors to spread the gospel of proper wilderness ethics. Kari and Joe's enthusiasm is contagious, which is why they are so effective as wilderness educators. Their message comes straight from the heart, and is well received by a diverse audience ranging from loggers in the Swan to children on a field trip.

To them wilderness education means making people more aware of what wildlands offer: solitude, clean air and water, a place for wildlife to roam freely, the spiritual connection. Joe marvels at how he has never sat down with anyone in the Wilderness who "didn't convey a sense of spiritual connection to the wildland—even the most redneck person imaginable." Recognizing that some people venture fearfully into the wilderness, Kari first shows them how they are benefited by wilderness so that they'll feel comfortable in the wild. Rejecting regulation in favor of education, the idea is to bring out the intrinsic goodness in every wilderness visitor, what causes him or her to enter the area in the first place.

Joe stresses that to be effective as wilderness educators they've got to "walk the talk" by being good role models. And speaking of walking, the two each walk an average of 1,500 miles during a four-and-a-half-month season in the Missions. Working far beyond their contract requirements, they are motivated by a love for wildlands and a commitment to the future. They see the future of wilderness education as a great opportunity for the Forest Service if the agency will only match rhetoric with dollars and action. At present, showing a commitment for wilderness does little to advance one's career within the agency. Kari and Joe would like to see a career track in wilderness management, whereby managers split the year between being rangers in the field and educators in schools and in-service training workshops. The delivery of wilderness education is failing within the Forest Service because foresters are not necessarily educators. The couple envision workshops that will teach managers how to teach. Summing up the importance of education, Kari states flatly that "if we don't do this now there won't be any wilderness."

LAND OWNERSHIP

- U.S. FOREST SERVICE (FS)
- U.S. NATIONAL PARK SERVICE (NPS)
- U.S. BUREAU OF LAND MANAGEMENT (BLM)
- U.S. FISH & WILDLIFE SERVICE (FWS)
- STATE OF MONTANA (MDFWP, S)
- TRIBAL (T)
- PRIVATE (P, TNC)
- DESIGNATED WILDERNESS AREAS AS OF FALL 1990

GARY D. HOLMES

THE "100,000 ACRE + CLUB" OF LARGE WILD AREAS

All or Part of Which Are in Montana

Rank by Size	Area Name	Contiguous Roadless Acreage in Montana	Major Ownership
1.	Bob Marshall Country	2,476,328	FS
2.	Absaroka-Beartooth Complex*	1,208,734	FS/NPS
3.	North Glacier*	575,000	NPS
4.	South Glacier	430,000	NPS
5.	Missouri Breaks Complex	407,492	BLM/FWS
6.	Selway-Bitterroot Complex*	383,421	FS
7.	Anaconda-Pintler/Sapphires	367,745	FS
8.	Gallatin Range*	263,440	FS/NPS
9.	Madison Range South*	242,696	FS
10.	West Pioneers	239,572	FS
11.	Cabinet Mountains Complex	186,872	FS
12.	Mission Mountains Complex	174,377	Tribal/FS
13.	Bighorn Mountains	150,000	Tribal
14.	East Pioneers	147,428	FS
15.	Crazy Mountains	136,547	FS/Private
16.	West Big Hole	133,977	FS
17.	Madison Range North	110,240	FS/BLM
18.	Snowcrest Range	110,000	FS/BLM/MDFWP
19.	Big Snowies	104,755	FS/BLM
20.	Stony Mountain	103,346	FS
21.	Allan Mountain*	102,386	FS
22.	Rattlesnake Wildlands Complex	101,000	FS/Tribal
23.	Great Burn[1]	98,680	FS
24.	Italian Peaks[2]	91,277	FS
25.	Blue Joint[3]	65,370	FS
26.	Line Creek Plateau[4]	20,680	FS

*Area contiguous to additional wildlands outside of Montana.

(1) Total Great Burn MT/ID wildland is 251,892 acres.
(2) Total Italian Peaks MT/ID wildland is 300,000 + acres.
(3) Contiguous to 2,361,761-acre Frank Church-River of No Return in Idaho.
(4) Total Line Creek Plateau MT/WY wildland is 112,800 acres.

Left: *Tahepia Lake in the Pioneers.*

THE WILDERNESS ACT

The single most important word in the landmark 1964 Wilderness Act is "enduring," in that the act's basic purpose is to provide an enduring resource of wilderness for this and future generations. Prior to 1964, the uncertain whim of administrative decree was all that protected wilderness, beginning in 1924 when part of the Gila National Forest became the first area so classified. During the 1930s, The Wilderness Society co-founder Bob Marshall saw wilderness "melting like a snowbank on a hot June day." Then in the 1950s Howard Zahniser of The Wilderness Society led a growing realization that "there ought to be a law," to achieve permanent protection of wildland. His worse fears materialized in 1963 when the Secretary of Agriculture declassified 240,000 acres of Idaho's Selway-Bitterroot Primitive Area in the upper Selway drainage (known as the Magruder Corridor)—a mistake that took 17 years to correct with the 1980 designation of the Frank Church-River of No Return Wilderness.

The act defines Wilderness as natural federal lands "where the earth and its community of life are untrammeled by man, where man is a visitor who does not remain." Wilderness opponents have interpreted the word "untrammeled" to mean that an area must be absolutely pure before it can qualify as Wilderness. A more accurate view is obtained by looking at the rest of the language, which states that Wilderness must "generally appear to have been affected primarily by the forces of nature, with the imprint of man's work substantially unnoticeable." The definition is thus qualified to reflect the reality that no area is absolutely "pure." Further, a Wilderness Area must have outstanding opportunities for solitude or primitive and unconfined recreation; and be at least 5,000 acres in size or large enough to preserve and use in an unimpaired state. Lastly, the area may contain ecological, geological, or other features of scientific, educational, scenic, or historical value.

Generally, Wilderness designation means that the land is protected from roads, timber harvest, motorized vehicles and equipment, and commercial uses except livestock grazing, development of pre-existing mining claims and leases, and outfitting. Exceptions exist for emergencies and administrative needs.

The Wilderness Act empowers three federal agencies to administer Wilderness: the National Park Service, the Fish and Wildlife Service, and the Forest Service. The 1976 Federal Land Policy and Management Act added the Bureau of Land Management to the list. Although these four agencies can make Wilderness recommendations, only Congress can designate Wilderness. Thus, by reserving this final authority, Congress has made the process of allocating wildland a matter of politics—which epitomizes our system of grass roots democracy. In the words of Bob Marshall, wild country is protected by "the organization of spirited people who will fight for the freedom of the wilderness." In Montana, we have come to view the process as "endless pressure endlessly applied."

JOHN REDDY

From Lincoln Peak, Glacier National Park.

BILL CUNNINGHAM

Above: *Ervin Ridge/Bullwhacker, Missouri Breaks.*
Right: *Russell Point near Utica.*

WILLIAM A. KOENIG

CHRONOLOGY

**Congressional Wildlands Allocation
and Roadless Area Inventories in Montana
Since Passage of the 1964 Wilderness Act**

1964—Wilderness Act signed into law establishing the National Wilderness Preservation System with automatic inclusion of the Bob Marshall, Selway-Bitterroot, Cabinet Mountains, Anaconda-Pintler, and Gates of the Mountains wilderness areas, along with mandated Wilderness review of the Spanish Peaks, Absaroka, and Beartooth primitive areas.
1972—Designation of the Scapegoat Wilderness.
1973—Completion of the original nationwide Forest Service roadless area inventory.
1975—Designation of the Mission Mountains Wilderness.
1976—Designation of the Red Rock Lakes, UL-Bend, and Medicine Lake national wildlife refuge wilderness areas, and the Elkhorns and Great Bear wilderness study areas.
1977—Passage of Senator Lee Metcalf's Montana Wilderness Study Act (S.393) which provided wilderness study status to Mt. Henry, Ten Lakes, Blue Joint, Sapphire, West Pioneers, Taylor-Hilgard, Hyalite-Porcupine-Buffalo Horn, Middle Fork Judith and Big Snowies "until otherwise determined by Congress."
1978—Designation of the Absaroka-Beartooth, Great Bear, east side addition to the Bob Marshall and Welcome Creek wilderness areas in three separate pieces of legislation.
1979—Release of the Forest Service second roadless area review and evaluation (RARE II), which stimulated the creation of state-wide Wilderness bills on a state-by-state basis.
1980—Designation of the Rattlesnake Wilderness and National Recreation Area.
1983—Designation of the Lee Metcalf Wilderness, with Bear Trap Canyon as the nation's first Bureau of Land Management Wilderness, the Cabin Creek Recreation and Wildlife Area, along with legislative release of the Mt. Henry Wilderness Study Area, portions of the Taylor-Hilgard Wilderness Study Area, and the Tongue River Breaks roadless area.

PRIMER ON WILDLAND ECONOMICS

Picture a dwindling resource that is increasingly sought by more and more people. You don't have to be an economist to understand the relationship between scarcity and value. If the supply of this resource is going down at a time when demand for it is going up, then it would certainly follow that the resource is becoming more valuable. Even though this oversimplified model ignores complex factors that are difficult to isolate, Montana's diminishing wild country is indeed such an increasingly valuable resource.

Simply and generally put, the best lands for development have long since been roaded, logged, mined and drilled. It stands to reason that the easiest, most accessible land yielding the highest quick return would be opened up first. Until recently, most of our remaining roadless lands have avoided the blade and saw because they have not been worth anyone's time or money to develop—a sort of internal self-protection provided by steep, rugged terrain, remoteness, and marginal commodity values. It would seem that if the cost of development, i.e. roads, exceeds the value of timber in an unroaded area, both short- and long-term, the area isn't going to be logged. Wrong. Public land management agencies, not accountable to the market, have little incentive to avoid below-cost development. In fact, quite the opposite is true, in that the incentive system within the Forest Service continues to reward managers when they spend tax dollars to meet production targets regardless of loss to the U.S. Treasury.

Virtually all timber sales planned as of this writing within Montana's unprotected roadless areas are below-cost. But the more important question is whether a given development project is below-benefit. If each project has to meet the test of positive net public benefit, then the loss of roadless values, including wildlife security, clean and stable water, scenic beauty, primitive recreation and wilderness would be weighed against the production of board feet of timber or of cubic feet of natural gas.

All of this points to a basic conclusion. Trading highly valued resources, such as wildlands, for lower-valued resources, such as below-cost timber, is bad public policy and even worse economics. Nowhere is this disparity in value greater than in Montana where millions of acres of the nation's finest unspoiled landscape face an uncertain future largely because of the possibility of development that is both-below-cost and below-benefit.

Tourism is the major arrow in an economic quiver increasingly used by conservationists in defense of wildland. Recently, the Montana Outfitters and Guides Association conducted a telephone survey of 57 outfitters who provide their services in proposed, but unprotected, wilderness areas. It was found that 50 Montana outfitter businesses depend on retaining 22 wild areas in their natural state. A 1986 Montana State University study determined that each outfitting business contributes $67,124 to Montana's economy. Therefore, the 50 dependent businesses are responsible for adding nearly $3.4 million to the state's economy while providing 282 jobs. These benefits accrue year after year from a renewable wildland base. Thus their loss should be balanced against the rotation cycle of timber harvest, which averages 100 years in Montana. Multiplying the annual economic impact by 100 gives a conservative estimate of long-term economic value in preserving these 22 roadless areas equal to nearly $340 million.

But University of Montana economist Dr. Thomas Power makes the convincing case that the primary economic benefit of wildland is not its value to others who travel from afar, hiring an outfitter. Rather, the major economic gain is to local people and to future generations who will live near these wildlands. The high quality environment of abundant, diverse wildlands in Montana nurtures Montanans in a way that makes them stay despite lower than average incomes. In this sense, the basis of wildland economics is not the commercial exchange of dollars of which tourism is a part, but the natural amenities that make Montana an attractive place in which to live and work. The love that people have for their local wildlands bespeaks an economic value already paid by their act and sacrifice of choosing to live here

TIM EGAN

Beartooth Mountains.

THE CABINET-YAAK

LEFT: JEFF GNASS; BELOW AND RIGHT: JOHN REDDY

Above: Yaak River.
Left: Ross Creek cedars define the eastern edge of the Scotchman Peaks wild area, rare ancient trees within a heavily logged area.
Facing page: Cabinet Mountains.

*I*slands of wildness in a sea of clearcuts: not very original, but an apt description of the roadless remnants in Montana's timber-rich northwest corner. These mountains, the Purcells, are drained by the Yaak River in a remote, low-elevation area of the state.

13

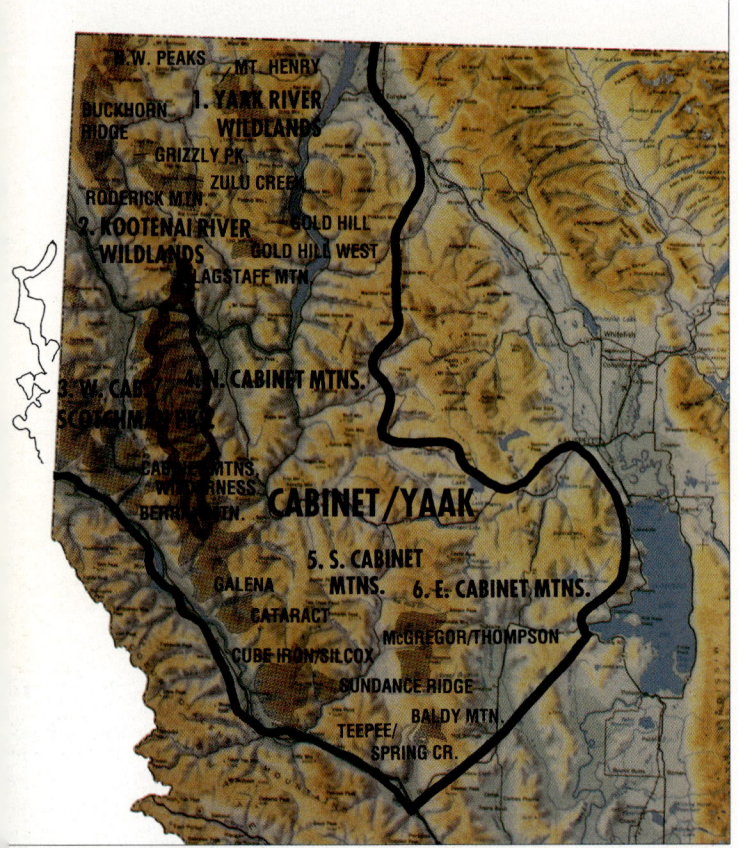

CABINET-YAAK WILDLANDS

Physiographic region COMPLEX Area Name	Area No.†	Montana Gross Acreage	Agency/ Ownership	Management Status
I. Cabinet/Yaak				
YAAK RIVER	1			
Northwest Peaks		20,330	FS	R-NW
Mt. Henry		12,000	FS	R-NW
Grizzly Peak		6,000	FS	R-NW
Buckhorn Ridge*		25,800	FS	R-NW
Zulu Creek		6,400	FS	R-NW
Roderick Mtn.		24,800	FS	R-NW
KOOTENAI RIVER	2			
Gold Hill		10,700	FS	R-NW
Gold Hill West		10,200	FS	R-NW
Flagstaff Mtn.		9,500	FS	R-NW
W. CABINETS/SCOTCHMAN PEAKS*	3	64,580	FS	R-NW
N. CABINET MTNS.	4			
Cabinet Mtns. Wilderness		94,272	FS	W
Contiguous lands		92,600	FS	R-NW
Berray Mtn.		8,600	FS	R-NW
(Contiguous Cabinet Mountains Wildlands: 186,872 acres)				
S. CABINET MTNS.	5			
Galena		17,500	FS	R-NW
Cataract		27,700	FS	R-NW
Cube Iron/Silcox		39,600	FS	R-NW
Sundance Ridge		9,440	FS	R-NW
Teepee/Spring Creek		15,250	FS	R-NW
E. CABINET MTNS.	6			
McGregor-Thompson		30,300	FS	R-NW
Baldy Mtn.		6,680	FS	R-NW

Total Wildlands: 532,252 acres. Wilderness: 94,272 acres (17.8%)

†For identification purposes in this book only
*Areas with contiguous wildlands in Idaho
**Areas with contiguous wildlands in Wyoming

KEY
Agency Symbols
BLM—Bureau of Land Management
FS—Forest Service
FWS—Fish & Wildlife Service
MDFWP—Montana Dept. of Fish, Wildlife & Parks
NPS—National Park Service
P—Private
S—State
SEA—USDA Science & Education Administration
T—Tribal
TNC—The Nature Conservancy

Management Status Symbols
ACEC—BLM Area of Critical Environmental Concern
BLM WSA—Bureau of Land Management Wilderness Study Area
FPA—Forest Service Further Planning Area
ISA—Instant BLM Study Area
NP—National Park
NRA—National Recreation Area
NWR—National Wildlife Refuge
ONA—BLM Outstanding Natural Area
PP—Private Preserve
R-NW—Roadless-Nonwilderness
RWMA—Recreation & Wildlife Management Area
SP—State Park
TPA—Tribal Primitive Area
TR—Tribal Reserve
TW—Tribal Wilderness
W—Wilderness
WMA—State Wildlife Management Area
WSA—Congressional Wilderness Study Area (Forest Service)

1 Yaak River Wildlands

The highest mountains in the Purcell Range are found in the 20,330-acre Northwest Peaks roadless area that drapes the slopes of a prominent north-south ridge where Montana touches Idaho and British Columbia. The tree-covered ridge attains its apex at 7,705' Northwest Peak. Here the remains of a 1930s lookout offer unlimited vistas of the surrounding Yaak River wildlands and far to the north into Canada. The alpine core of the area is managed by the Kootenai National Forest as a Scenic Area. Moderate glaciation has carved pockets for seven high lakes, three of which support rainbow and cutthroat trout.

Solitude abounds in secluded upper West Fork Yaak basins where a diverse forest of whitebark pine, spruce, subalpine fir, alpine larch, western redcedar and hemlock is home to deer, elk, moose and an occasional grizzly bear.

Twenty miles to the east across a maze of roads and clearcuts rises another prominent Purcell Peak—Mt. Henry—the most distinctive feature of what was once a 23,450-acre Congressional Wilderness Study Area. Mt. Henry was released to nonwilderness uses as part of the 1983 Lee Metcalf Wilderness bill. Today, the rocky point of Mt. Henry rises to 7,243' above a thick forest of mostly lodgepole pine. Steep rocky cliffs rise above seven tiny lakes along the Mt. Henry-Boulder Mountain ridgeline. Timber sales in Turner and Vinal creeks have reduced this wildland to a remnant of the remnant.

To the southwest, across another 15 miles of forest development, lies the compact 6,000-acre Grizzly Peak roadless area, which encompasses the pine-covered slopes and cedar-hemlock bottoms of Grizzly Creek. The main ridge—from 6,400' Clark Mountain east to 6,100' Grizzly Peak—offers grassy campsites, expansive views of the Purcell/Yaak River country, and prime mule deer habitat. The broad grassy mound of Grizzly Peak offers a central panorama of all the Yaak River wildlands.

Westward, a few miles beyond the Yaak River and immediately across Spread Creek from Northwest Peaks, stretch 25 miles of roadless ridge that parallels and defines a segment of the north-south Montana-Idaho boundary. Some 25,800 acres of the 31,600-acre Buckhorn Ridge roadless area are within Montana, as is most of the wildland's namesake topographic feature. Rising between 6,000' and 6,500', the ridge is broad and open with grassy sideslopes dropping steeply into forested basins divided by spur ridges.

As part of the Cabinet-Yaak Grizzly Bear Ecosystem, Buckhorn Ridge is as important to the great bear as it is to summering deer, elk and moose in lush subalpine valleys, despite the closeness of forest roads on all sides.

Across the Yaak River only a few miles east are two of the remaining six roadless vestiges of the Yaak—Roderick Mountain and Zulu Creek, separated by the South Fork of the Yaak. The 6,400-acre Zulu Creek area is a rarity. Apart from a gently climbing ridgeline from Pipe Creek Summit to 6,597' Pink Mountain, Zulu Creek is rolling timberland—very much like the surrounding cutover lands. Grizzly bears find refuge in this small but diverse landscape, from the Douglas-fir slopes of Pink Mountain, to dense spruce-fir stream bottoms, to potholes and wet meadows in the southern portion.

To the immediate west is the wild centerpiece and most productive grizzly habitat in the Yaak—the 24,800-acre Roderick Mountain roadless area. This landscape of forested, moderately steep slopes and low-elevation creek bottoms is dominated by the 6,644' summit after which the area is named and by the 4,900' Independence Mountain ridgeline along the northwestern edge. Moose winter on the southern exposures above Seventeen Mile Creek and the long, straight faultline of Flattail Creek.

2   Kootenai River Wildlands

Three small roadless enclaves comprising 30,400 acres, surrounded by extensive forest development, are the last of the Kootenai River wild country.

In the 10,700-acre Gold Hill roadless area, steep, heavily vegetated streams, separated by tree-covered feeder ridges, drain to the west shore of Koocanusa Reservoir. Rock bluffs contrast with the flat bottoms of Parsnip Creek where large numbers of whitetail and mule deer browse.

Timber sales in the early 1980s bisected the original Gold Hill roadless land, leaving the 10,200-acre Gold Hill West area to the southwest. Here a forest of dense lodgepole pine is wild enough to support a wandering grizzly, with the only evidence of human use being a primitive trail up the West Branch of the South Fork of Big Creek. A moose standing in a beaver pond is a common sight in the West Branch.

The gentle slopes of 6,168' Lost Soul Mountain on the east end change to the steeper terrain of Gold Hill Mountain in the west half. To the south the scenic canyon of Noisy Creek invites hidden discoveries.

The rugged southern face of the 9,500-acre Flagstaff Mountain roadless area overlooks the Kootenai River near historic Kootenai Falls. In the spring here, bighorn sheep are often spotted from Highway 2. Peaks above 6,000', including 6,075' Flagstaff Mountain, dominate the ridgetops and open grassland sidehills surrounding the West Fork of

BILL CUNNINGHAM

Buckhorn Ridge south from Keno Mountain.

Quartz Creek. This drainage is highlighted by a combination of old growth spruce and fir and a large, open burn.

Future logging is planned for more than half of these vanishing Kootenai River wildlands.

The Cabinet Mountains are the major range of northwest Montana, so much so that they almost seem out of place with respect to the surrounding lower, more subdued country. They stretch for more than 100 miles from northwest to southeast. From the Kootenai River on the north, the Cabinets are bounded by the Idaho line to the west, the Clark Fork River on the south, and the Flathead Indian Reservation to the east. This vast mountain system can be broken down into the western, northern, southern and eastern Cabinets, each of which includes distinctive wild country.

3 *Western Cabinets: Scotchman Peaks*

The wildest and least developed land in the Cabinets may well be the 86,250-acre Scotchman Peaks roadless area, which extends from Idaho's panhandle to Montana's Bull River. Although the Montana peaks barely reach 6,500', the rugged landscape contains striking glacial cirques at the head of Savage and Ross creeks.

Above the cirque headwalls, hillsides of alpine vegetation drop sharply into the West Fork of Blue Creek—while the south slopes of dramatic Sawtooth and Billiard Table mountains send snowmelt through parks and down waterfalls to the East Fork of Blue Creek. Northward, the U-shaped valley of the South Fork of Ross Creek winds through meadows and rockslides to stately stands of ancient hemlock and white pine, cutting through a jumble of moss-covered boulders and devil's club to the majestic Ross Creek cedar grove—home of the largest western redcedar still standing in northwest Montana.

For 10 miles the rocky south slopes of Pellick Ridge fall nearly 4,000 feet into the Clark Fork and lower Bull River valleys. The cooler north aspects of the ridge display a continuous canopy of trees down to the lower canyons. Pellick Ridge offers superlative vistas as well as room to roam for grizzly bears, bighorn sheep, goats and elk. Cutthroat trout dwell in Scotchman's only named lake—Little Spar.

The 64,580 acres of Scotchman Peaks in Montana are unusual in that the area has remained roadless to the very edge of its natural landform—from peaks to valleys.

BUD JOURNEY

4 Northern Cabinet Mountains

The 8,600-acre Berray Mountain roadless area sits opposite Pellick Ridge between the south and east forks of the Bull River. A lookout atop 6,150' Berray Mountain and a few miles of trail are the only evidence of past human use. High forested ridges distinguish the country in the north, with steep cliffs and sparse forests to the south and west. These sunny exposures present the Kootenai Naitonal Forest's best viewing opportunity of wintering bighorn sheep, elk and deer.

The 94,272-acre Cabinet Mountains Wilderness occupies the higher elevations of the northern range of the Cabinets about 15 miles southwest of Libby. A narrow line of snowcapped peaks, glacial lakes, valleys cut by icy streams, and cascading waterfalls runs north-south for 40 twisting, up and down miles.

Two major north-south ridges divide the north Cabinets, sending Lake Creek north to the Kootenai River while spilling the Bull River south to the Clark Fork. A dramatic mile of vertical relief separates lush stream bottoms from the rocky crest of centrally-located Snowshoe Peak—the high point of the range at 8,738'. These rugged pinnacles challenge technical climbers in a primeval setting.

From an ancient shallow sea, sedimentary basins were thrust upward here. After the mountains were built they were shaped by widespread glaciation, resulting in today's wonderland of sharp ridges, more than 80 cirque lakes, wet meadows, hanging valleys, U-shaped drainages and scoured slopes.

As the highest mountain barrier directly east of the Cascades, the Cabinets receive up to 100 inches of annual precipitation, with snow depths exceeding 800 inches in high, sheltered basins. This maritime influence produces vegetation on every acre, from old-growth cedar and hemlock to delicate little harebells blooming from rock fissures in September.

Denizens of the Wilderness include wolverine, deer, elk, moose, mountain sheep, goat, black bear and a small but threatened population of grizzly bears that survive despite development pressures from nearby roads, logging and mining. Potential large-scale mining, permitted by a "grandfather" clause in the 1964 Wilderness Act, is likely in the southern, narrow Rock Creek portion of this linear Wilderness. With most trails only three to five miles in length dead-ending in a high basin, the impact of industrial mining on solitude and other wilderness values could be profound.

Contiguous wildlands almost equal in size to the designated Wilderness—92,600 acres—encircle the Cabinet Wilderness on all sides. Five roadless clusters result in a single wildland in the northern range of 186,872 acres.

The east face extends the length of the range in a row of rugged canyons, from which the Cabinet Mountains get their name. Topographic relief is nearly 5,000 feet from dark old-growth stream bottoms to rocky pinnacles above 7,000'.

A roadless band of forested sidehills averaging a mile in width runs for 16 miles along the northwest face. Mountain goats winter in Camp Creek and in the dramatic Goat Rocks, with bighorn sheep common near Ibex Peak.

A fringe of roadless country around Government Mountain juts out to the Bull River from the west-central Wilderness boundary. Mosaics of conifers and hardwoods from the 1910 Burn provide excellent forage for both grizzly bears and wintering elk.

The southwest face, containing McKay and Swamp creeks, is irreplaceable range for mule deer and grizzlies in

PETE & ALICE BENGEYFIELD

Above: *Leigh Lake in the Cabinet Mountains.*

Facing page: *Thunderstorm over the Cabinets, from Bull River.*

LEFT: PAT O'HARA; BELOW: JEFF FOOTT

the fall. A delightful streamside trail up Swamp Creek is unique in the Cabinets because of its length.

5 Southern Cabinet Mountains

The mountains of the southern range are lower and less jagged than their northern neighbors. A transmission line splits off the 17,500-acre Galena roadless area from Swamp Creek and the Cabinet Mountains Wilderness. Open ridges span out in every direction from the area's high point—6,326' Canyon Peak, which sits at the head of the pristine drainages of Galena, Canyon and Silver Butte creeks. Grizzly, elk and numerous mule deer roam the steep ponderosa pine- and Douglas-fir–clad hillsides.

Just south of the Vermilion River is a 27,700-acre wildland of severely rugged cliffs, talus and vertical rock ribs called Cataract after its major drainage. Cataract Creek is a hanging valley watershed so remote that even the lower reaches near the Vermilion River road provide deep solitude. Native cutthroat trout abound, as well as a sizeable resident elk herd. Tiny alpine lakes along the Seven Point-Vermilion ridge are barren of fish but ideal for primitive camping and hiking.

The centerpiece of the Southern Cabinets is 39,600 acres of roadless high lake country bounded by 7,429' Mt. Headley, Cube Iron Mountain, and 4,500 feet of vertical relief from the Clark Fork Valley to Mt. Silcox. Beyond the steep, open Douglas-fir–covered hillsides seen from nearby Thompson Falls lies an incredible array of glaciated peaks, lake-studded alpine basins, old-growth stands of ancient conifers, and clear, rushing streams. Few wild places in Montana contain such a compact representation of landforms, vegetation and resulting wildlife, including grizzlies, cougars, lynx and bobcats.

More than 20 drainages fan out like spokes on a wheel from the main divide. A few of these streams still harbor the right combination of fine gravels and shady habitat to support a relict population of native cutthroat and bull trout. Sedimentation from a vast road network, especially on the east side, has all but wiped out the once-impressive spawning runs of bulls.

To the immediate east, across the West Fork Thompson River, Sundance Ridge winds through a 9,440-acre roadless area apexing at 7,004' Priscilla Peak. The ridge is dotted with brushy parks, rock outcrops, and open clumps of whitebark pine and mountain hemlock.

To the south, 15,250 acres of steep slopes, dense forest and rugged terrain make up the Teepee-Spring Creek roadless area. Northwest-trending faults skirt interior ridges, sending streams outward in all four compass directions.

east-west streams and divides fan out like teeth on a comb. A hike up one of the deeply-cut valleys may yield trout, scenic views of rock strata and formations, and perhaps a glimpse of a moose, marten, or pileated woodpecker.

Baldy Mountain, at 7,500', dominates its namesake 6,680-acre roadless surroundings. Open rock ledges, scree slopes, an active lookout, and a national recreation trail mark the summit. Two tiny subalpine lakes nestle on the north side of the peak, with rainbow-stocked Baldy Lake hidden in trees to the southeast.

BILL CUNNINGHAM

6 Eastern Cabinet Mountains

The eastern extension of the Cabinets ends just east of the Thompson River with only two small national forest areas surviving in a wild state. The "McGregor" part of the once-86,000-acre McGregor-Thompson roadless area has recently been roaded and logged, leaving a remnant wildland of 30,300 acres.

The eastern boundary is a north-to-northeast 6,000' to 7,000' ridge that borders the Flathead Indian Reservation. From this single connecting ridgeline, a series of parallel

Cabinet-Yaak Wildlands: 532,252 acres
Designated Wilderness: 94,272 acres (1 area)—17.8% of total

Above: Toward Mt. Silcox from Cube Iron Peak.

Facing page, left: "A" Peak and Granite Lake in the Cabinets. Right Pileated woodpecker.

19

GREATER GLACIER/ BOB MARSHALL COUNTRY

LEFT: PAT O'HARA; BELOW: ERWIN & PEGGY BAUER; RIGHT: GEORGE WUERTHNER

The northern Continental Divide forms the spine of Montana's wilderness heartland in a pristine mountain fastness that defies superlatives. One of three of the state's wild acres is within a compact "Crown of the Continent" region that stretches from the 49th parallel south to Rogers Pass and from the verdant Whitefish Range east to the dry, windswept Front Range of the Rockies. This is wilderness at its best, in large enough chunks to preserve intact ecosystems and complete landforms, healthy wildlife populations and mysteries of genetic diversity that may hold the key to human survival on earth.

Above: Mt. Field, the Rocky Mountain Front.
Left: Paintbrush.

Facing page: Prairie Reef in the Lewis and Clark National Forest.

21

GLACIER/ BOB MARSHALL COUNTRY

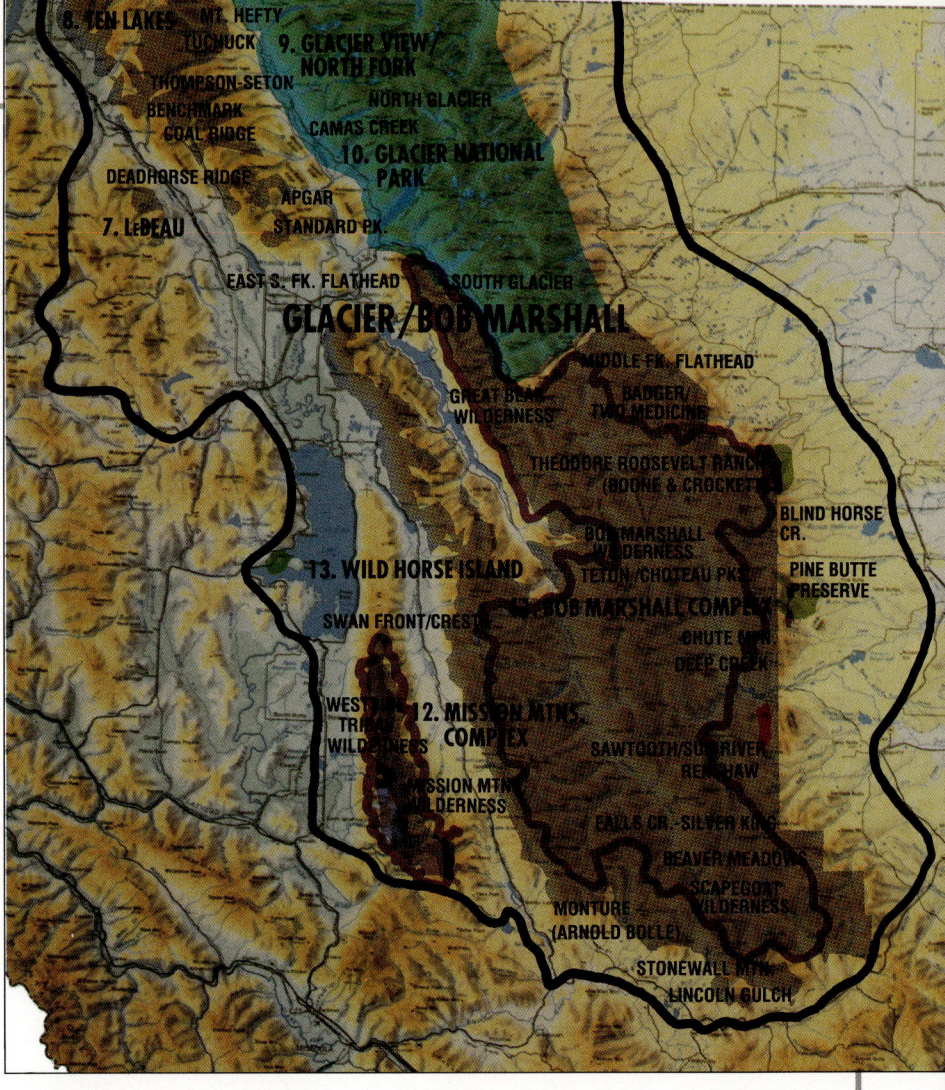

Physiographic region COMPLEX Area Name	Area No.†	Montana Gross Acreage	Agency/ Ownership	Management Status
II. Glacier/Bob Marshall				
LeBeau	7	6,210	FS	R-NW
Ten Lakes	8	43,900	FS	WSA, R-NW
Glacier View/North Fork	9			
Mt. Hefty		13,720	FS	R-NW
Tuchuck		19,820	FS	R-NW
Thompson-Seton		83,840	FS	R-NW
Benchmark		6,490	FS	R-NW
Coal Ridge		16,480	FS	R-NW
Deadhorse Ridge		27,150	FS/State	R-NW
Standard Peak		7,770	FS	R-NW
Glacier National Park	10			
North Glacier		575,000	NPS/T	NP/T
South Glacier		430,000	NPS/T	NP/T
Apgar		33,000	NPS	NP
Camas Creek		13,500	NPS	NP
Bob Marshall Complex	11			
Great Bear Wilderness		286,700	FS	W
Bob Marshall Wilderness		1,009,356	FS	W
Scapegoat Wilderness		239,296	FS	W
East South Fork Flathead		57,640	FS	R-NW
Middle Fork Flathead		42,450	FS	R-NW
Badger/Two Medicine		120,000	FS	R-NW
Teton River High Peaks		77,572	FS/MDFWP	R-NW, WMA, PP, ONA, BLM/TNC/P
Deep Creek		52,329	FS/BLM	FPA, ONA
Renshaw		57,611	FS	R-NW
Falls Creek-Silver King		75,417	FS	R-NW
Rocky Mtn. Front Contiguous		30,000	P/S	R-NW
Stonewall Mtn.		51,537	FS	R-NW
Monture		104,100	FS/MDFWP	R-NW, WMA
Swan Front/Crest		272,320	FS/S	R-NW
(Contiguous Bob Marshall Complex Wild Area: 2,476,328 acres)				
Sawtooth/Sun River		20,500	FS/MDFWP	R-NW, WMA
Lincoln Gulch		8,125	FS	R-NW
Mission Mtns. Complex	12			
Mission Mtns. Wilderness		73,877	FS	W
Contiguous lands		11,000	FS/S	R-NW
Westside Tribal Wilderness		89,500	T	TW
(Contiguous Mission Mtns. Wildlands: 174,377 acres)				
Wild Horse Island	13	2,100	MDFWP	SP

Total Wildlands: 3,958,310 acres. Wilderness: 1,698,729 acres (42.9%)

†For identification purposes in this book only
*Areas with contiguous wildlands in Idaho
**Areas with contiguous wildlands in Wyoming

KEY
Agency Symbols
BLM—Bureau of Land Management
FS—Forest Service
FWS—Fish & Wildlife Service
MDFWP—Montana Dept. of Fish, Wildlife & Parks
NPS—National Park Service
P—Private
S—State
SEA—USDA Science & Education Administration
T—Tribal
TNC—The Nature Conservancy

Management Status Symbols
ACEC—BLM Area of Critical Environmental Concern
BLM WSA—Bureau of Land Management Wilderness Study Area
FPA—Forest Service Further Planning Area
ISA—Instant BLM Study Area
NP—National Park
NRA—National Recreation Area
NWR—National Wildlife Refuge
ONA—BLM Outstanding Natural Area
PP—Private Preserve
R-NW—Roadless-Nonwilderness
RWMA—Recreation & Wildlife Management Area
SP—State Park
TPA—Tribal Primitive Area
TR—Tribal Reserve
TW—Tribal Wilderness
W—Wilderness
WMA—State Wildlife Management Area
WSA—Congressional Wilderness Study Area (Forest Service)

7 LeBeau

In some respects the tiny 6,210-acre LeBeau roadless area is a microcosm of the larger wildland region in which it is located. Undulating wetlands and meadows are surrounded by a dense matrix of western larch, lodgepole and ponderosa pine, birch, aspen and many young western redcedars. The higher country exhibits steep glaciated rock formations that tower above eight small lakes. This wild enclave is rough enough to discourage development and remote enough to attract black bear, cougar, moose, elk and deer.

8 Ten Lakes

With British Columbia as its northern border, the 43,900-acre Ten Lakes Montana Wilderness Study Act Area resembles a giant starfish. Its roadless tentacles wrap around developed lands that were salvage-logged after the 1950s spruce bark beetle epidemic. From glaciated Therriault Pass north, an alpine core of clear lakes, lush mountain meadows, rocky peaks, talus slopes, gnarled subalpine larch and whitebark pine, and bare ridges lends a distinctive alpine flavor to this last vestige of western Whitefish Range wild country. A broad array of habitats from gentle, forested foothills to glacial basins invites a corresponding diversity of wildlife. Elk, moose, black bear and deer are plentiful. Less common is the occasional grizzly bear, wolf, or perhaps the woodland caribou hidden in the security of old-growth forests. The remoteness of Ten Lakes is deepened, literally, by more than 12 feet of snow in high, sheltered cirques. My favorite memories of the country include hoary marmots darting around rock gardens of talus and colorful alpine flowers, with hearty little rosy finches flitting overhead.

9 Glacier View/North Fork Wildlands

The 50-mile-long Whitefish Range, from Columbia Falls north to the Canadian line, is a living storehouse of wildness, despite being riddled by logging roads. From British Columbia to the edge of the Big Mountain ski resort, seven wildlands encompass 175,270 acres of untamed forested peaks and basins averaging 7,000' in elevation. With 90 percent of the country draining to the Wild and Scenic North Fork Flathead River, and facing east to Glacier Park, these unroaded portions of the Whitefish Mountains are collectively the Glacier View/North Fork Wildlands.

The security and lush productivity of these remote forests provide some of the most densely occupied grizzly bear habitat in North America. With an abundant prey base of whitetail deer, elk, moose and, perhaps, even the rare mountain caribou, these wildlands are also being colonized by descendants of the famed "Magic Pack" of wolves, now reproducing on the U.S. side of the border as the Camas Pack.

Beginning with the 13,720-acre Mt. Hefty country on the British Columbia border, the northern trio of undeveloped lands totaling 117,380 acres is commonly known as the North Fork Wildlands. At 7,585', the north face of glaciated Mt. Hefty slopes into Canada. Steep canyons studded with caves cut through gently rolling moraines. Large, intense fires during the early part of the century account for today's thick forests of lodgepole pine and western larch, with whitebark pine and subalpine fir the rule above 6,000'.

Telltale marks of past glaciation are even more evident in the secluded 19,820-acre Tuchuck roadless area, where cirque headwalls rise steeply above narrow alpine canyons. Cutthroat fin the icy waters of one of six tiny lakes near the head of Thoma Creek. At least 50 elk summer in moist basins studded with subalpine larch and fir. A blend of unique geology and vegetation makes the Tuchuck drainage ideal for research into natural processes.

Mt. Thompson-Seton and its namesake 83,840-acre wild area are named for the turn-of-the-century naturalist who co-founded the Boy Scouts of America. Jagged Krag and Krinklehorn peaks on the west side are dubbed for characters in Seton's well-known children's story, "Krag, the Kootenai Ram." The lobe of wild country south of heavily developed Whale Creek is dominated by the high point of the range, rounded 8,086' Nasukoin Mountain, which is encircled by 15 subalpine lakes, including fish-filled Chain Lakes. East-face rock cliffs of 7,814' Lake Mountain tower above a sheltered lake still frozen in July. A prominent ridge to Nasukoin looks into secret basins perfect for foraging grizzlies. Subalpine larch grows here in every form imaginable, from gnarled and windblown to stately tall

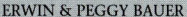

Male black bear.

BILL CUNNINGHAM

The North Fork wildlands near Nasukoin Mountain are among the most densely occupied grizzly habitat in Montana

trees. Glacier lilies abound, as does another kind of lily—beargrass. Ridges and peaks possess the split personality of being rounded on one side, and rough-hewn with cliff faces, on the other. And always, there is the profound presence of Glacier Park to the east. The lower, more subdued mountains of these wildlands are a pleasing contrast to their higher, more rugged neighbors across the North Fork.

The 6,490-acre Benchmark roadless area is a lofty, rocky east-west divide on both sides of 7,099' Benchmark Peak. Ridges of open whitebark pine are draped with hillsides of beargrass and subalpine fir. Shrub-covered lower slopes near Red Meadow Lake provide one of the North Fork's most glorious explosions of fall colors.

From 7,305' Diamond Peak on the Whitefish Divide, the 16,480-acre Coal Ridge roadless area extends eastward for 10 miles along high, rugged ridgetops with rock outcrops and scattered whitebark pine. Grizzlies and lynx stalk through open coniferous forests, small grassy meadows, and tiny potholes sheltered below the divide.

Deadhorse Ridge is the most pronounced feature in its namesake 27,150-acre roadless area, which includes 3,600 acres of contiguous wildlands in the west-side Stillwater State Forest and east-side Coal Creek State Forest. The alpine western boundary along the main Whitefish Divide from Haines Pass south to Werner Peak is traversed by about eight miles of the Ralph Thayer Memorial National Recreation Trail. Irregularly shaped by road systems on all sides, unroaded fingers extend east toward the North Fork for 13 miles. Lower country near Langford Creek is vital winter range for elk and mule deer.

Still more high, rocky, rugged ridges form the backbone of the 7,770-acre Standard Peak roadless area—the most southerly of the Glacier View/North Fork Wildlands. This small unroaded pocket serves as critically needed security for grizzly bears in a major travel corridor between Apgar Mountain in Glacier and the Whitefish Divide.

Mt. Hefty, Tuchuck, Thompson-Seton and the smaller, more fragmented North Fork Wildlands to the south exemplify a wild complex whose whole is greater than the sum of its seven parts. Rare and endangered wilderness-dependent predators—grizzlies and wolves—recognize and rely upon this greater whole.

10 Glacier National Park Wildlands

Glacier National Park is America's premier wilderness park, with 1,006,500 of its 1,013,100 acres remaining wild and free in four roadless units. The Continental Divide separates Glacier's spectacular back country into two nearly equal parts, and is itself bisected by a road in only one location, the Going-to-the-Sun Highway at Logan Pass. This "land of shining mountains" was molded by fire, torrential rains, internal pressures and the great continental ice sheets to produce a million-acre wilderness with more than 200 gemlike tarns, distinctive elongated lakes, countless waterfalls, vertical relief of a mile or more in some valleys, and broad U-shaped drainages. The grinding rivers of ice that melted some 10,000 years ago left an ongoing record of the forces of erosion and glaciation on sedimentary rock. These thick Precambrian formations appear as broad bands of greens, reds and other distinctive colors in the landscape.

Upon this jagged and varied land live some 1,200 plant species, at least 200 kinds of birds and about 60 species of mammals. The grizzly and colonizing wolf require the security afforded by Glacier's wild terrain, thick vegetation and inaccessibility. The variety of flora and fauna stems from five undisturbed life zones. From the equivalent of polar ice and snow high along the Great Divide, one can descend into alpine tundra, primeval coniferous forest, deciduous forest and grassland.

WOLVES IN THE NORTH FORK

It was late April 1986 when a wolf den at Sullivan Meadows on the Glacier National Park side of the North Fork became the site of a historic event in the annals of wild happenings. The dominant male and female of the "Magic Pack" of re-colonizing wolves became the proud parents of a five-pup litter—the first documented birth of wolves in the western United States in more than half a century. Years earlier, a large, black three-toed male was sighted and later identified as the sire of a 1982 litter born just north of the border. The newly-formed pack would appear and disappear as if by magic.

In the spring of 1987, the Magic Pack split into the Camas and Sage Creek packs, but the latter group was virtually wiped out by fall of that year. The Camas pack of nine adults continues to hunt the North Fork despite the loss of its 1989 litter from disease. The spring of 1990 witnessed the birth of two wolf litters south of the border. The Camas Pack denned and produced a litter north of Polebridge near its 1986 den. The second litter came into the world at Sullivan Meadows from a female that had split off from the Camas Pack.

Why is the North Fork being re-colonized by wolves? As much as anything it may simply have been the chance encounter at the right time between a male and female. As a result, Greater Glacier is the only ecosystem in the western U.S. with *the* major predator. The highly social wolf affects the ecosystem far more than solitary predators such as mountain lions. According to Wolf Ecology Project Director Bob Ream, "wolves are the missing link in most of Montana's wild country. When they move into the Bob, the Wilderness will be complete." Field researchers working for the project are gathering vital information about how wolves use a Rocky Mountain ecosystem while conducting long-term monitoring of this endangered species from the very beginning of its re-entry into the wilds of Montana.

ERWIN & PEGGY BAUER

North Glacier is the largest of the four wild areas at 575,000 acres, which includes 30,000 acres along the eastern slopes of the Lewis Range on the Blackfeet Reservation. Only two contiguous wildlands in Montana exceed North Glacier in size. This untamed region continues into Canada's Waterton Park as the most remote country in Glacier. The north end is crowned by the park's highest point—10,448' Mt. Cleveland. With a rise of 6,700 feet in only four miles, the impressive north face of Cleveland has the highest and steepest vertical ascent in all of Montana's wildlands. A portion of the lightning-caused 1988 Red Bench fire in the North Fork burned intensely into the Quartz-Logging Creek region of North Glacier. The area presents an excellent opportunity to study fire's ecological effects in a wilderness environment.

BRUCE SELYEM

Above: *Coal Creek drainage and Mt. St. Nicholas, Glacier National Park.*

Facing page: *Mt. Reynolds.*

The 430,000-acre South Glacier roadless area includes 15,000 acres of foothill country on the Blackfeet Reservation, which makes it Montana's fourth-largest wildland. This 25-by-35-mile primitive expanse is a wonderland of alpine lakes and lofty pinnacles, including fabled Triple Divide that gives birth to three ocean watersheds.

The Apgar Mountains contain some of Glacier's best grizzly habitat within a 33,000-acre roadless area sandwiched between the North Fork Flathead River and the Camas Creek road. To the immediate north is the elongated 13,500-acre Camas Creek roadless area which stretches from Apgar to above Logging Creek. Sullivan Meadow along the northern boundary is the den site of American-born wolves from the Camas Pack.

It is ironic but perhaps merciful that Glacier's 1,051,500 acres of wildlands are so formidable that more than 98 percent of park visitors are content to view them from a comfortable distance as they drive over Logan Pass.

11 Bob Marshall Wilderness Complex

If there is any widely accepted sacred ground in Montana it is the revered Bob Marshall Country—flagship of our nation's Wilderness "fleet". Affectionately dubbed "the Bob," this largest of Montana's wildlands is a remarkable unroaded expanse of 2,476,328 acres. The contiguous Great Bear, Bob Marshall and Scapegoat wilderness areas make up the 1,535,352-acre core of the complex that has been formally designated Wilderness. The remaining unprotected band of nearly 1 million acres encircles the core like a giant horseshoe and is part of the Bob in the minds of most people. Indeed, peripheral wildlands in the Swan Face and east-side Rocky Mountain Front harbor the wildest and least visited country in the entire ecosystem.

The name honors the tireless "commanding general" of the American wilderness movement, who created a legacy of wildland preservation, writings and monumental treks before his untimely death in 1939. More than 140 miles without a road separate Marias Pass on the north from Rogers Pass to the south, making the center of the Bob by far the most remote country in Montana in terms of distance from the nearest road.

This profile of the Bob Marshall Country begins with the three wilderness areas in one. Then the contiguous lands are dealt with as subregions, clockwise from the east side of the South Fork Flathead River, recognizing that each is part of a greater whole. The Bob Marshall subregions in the order of presentation are:

  Great Bear Wilderness—286,700 acres
  Bob Marshall Wilderness—1,009,356 acres
  Scapegoat Wilderness—239,296 acres
  East South Fork Flathead—57,640 acres
  Middle Fork Flathead—42,450 acres
  Badger-Two Medicine—120,000 acres
  Teton River High Peaks—77,572 acres
  Deep Creek—52,329 acres
  Renshaw—57,611 acres
  Falls Creek-Silver King—75,417 acres
  Contiguous state & private land along Rocky Mountain Front—30,000 acres
  Stonewall Mountain—51,537 acres
  Swan Front-Swan Crest—272,320 acres
Total Bob Marshall contiguous lands: 2,476,328 acres

Great Bear Wilderness—The 286,700-acre Great Bear Wilderness encompasses the entire upper drainage of the Middle Fork Flathead River from the Continental Divide westward to the rugged Flathead Range. Knife ridges along the divide give way to heavily forested mountainsides, gently-sloping meadows, and open river-bottom parks. Glacial action, which created U-shaped valleys and cirques, determined the present topography and drainage patterns.

As the surging lifeline of a great wilderness watershed, the Middle Fork is Montana's wildest river. Old timers called it Big River and the trail that parallels it still goes by that name. The Big River begins modestly as a drop of melting snow on the steep slope of a Great Divide mountain, where a glacier once rode the landscape. As a tiny rivulet it tumbles down hillsides through shady spruce bogs and subalpine meadows. Countless other tributaries enter the Big River. This is a stream of constantly changing moods, from placid emerald pools so clear that the spots can be counted on the backs of native cutthroat to frenzied rushes of white foam hellbent for the Pacific.

Migratory herds of elk move great distances between summer and winter ranges, with south-facing benches along the Middle Fork hosting up to 600 head of wintering wapiti. But more than anything, it was the free-roaming grizzly that inspired Senator Lee Metcalf to achieve preservation of this northern habitat link between the Bob and Glacier Park.

Bob Marshall Wilderness—The most remote reaches of the 1,009,356-acre Bob Marshall Wilderness are along the serpentine spine of the Great Divide—the heart of which is the fabled Chinese Wall. This imposing limestone precipice, towering 1,000 feet for 13 miles, is the soaring backdrop for the annual fall pageant of lovesick bugling bull elk competing for their harems. The climatic barrier of the Continental Divide influences vegetation, wildlife, and the nature of the land itself. Moist Pacific maritime weather on the west side—with lush, diverse forest—changes dramatically to drier, more open country to the east. Major streams emanate from the divide, including the blue ribbon South Fork Flathead, which gets its start in the broad meadows and willow bottoms of Danaher Basin. East of the Divide the vast Sun River drainage includes a 200,000-acre wilderness game preserve that the Montana legislature closed to hunting in 1913 to maintain the aboriginal Sun River elk herd of some 3,000 migratory animals. The Bob is the last great stronghold of the silvertip grizzly, that threatened symbol of true wilderness. The ultimate wilderness sight is one of these magnificent wilderness-dependent beasts ambling along the rock-strewn base of the Chinese Wall in search of wild parsnips, marmots and other tasty morsels. Other seldom-seen inhabitants include the wolverine, mountain lion, and even the endangered gray wolf.

Although composed mostly of alternating river valleys and north-south mountain ranges, the Bob Marshall also contains more than 100 lakes, the largest of which is 4½-mile-long Big Salmon. Other key features that symbolize this untamed expanse include the trailless Flathead Alps, the 20-mile-long anticline of the secluded White River, and

JOHN REDDY

BILL CUNNINGHAM PHOTOS

that northern sentinel of the Bob—8,890' Silvertip Mountain—site of one of the nation's deepest cave systems.

Scapegoat Wilderness—The highest point on the Continental Divide within Bob Marshall country is massive 9,202' Scapegoat Mountain, the majestic centerpiece of a 239,296-acre Wilderness that bears its name. The Wilderness straddles both sides of the Great Divide, with the headwaters of the Dearborn River and Falls Creek rising on the east, and various forks of the Big Blackfoot River to the west. The awesome 1,000' limestone cliffs of Scapegoat, stretching nearly four miles along the east face of the massif, are a southern extension of the Chinese Wall. Scattered subalpine forests of spruce, whitebark pine and fir open to grassy parks and gently sloping meadows highlighted by the rough-hewn signatures of old burns. The twisting, up-and-down nature of the Continental Divide is especially striking when viewed from the Scapegoat plateaus.

Several years ago I made a tricky scramble up the loose rock of an avalanche chute to the summit of Scapegoat. I needed to concentrate intensely, so there was no time to admire the scenery on the way up. I was thus doubly surprised to find myself eyeball-to-eyeball with a large mountain goat on a ledge only a few yards above me. Minutes later I spotted two circling golden eagles—one of the few natural predators of goats, which are otherwise secure in their cliff domain. From the main plateau I watched a herd of elk feeding in a remote basin far below. On the way down I jumped a pair of large muley bucks at the jumbled head of the Dearborn. A grizzly turning rocks in the talus for insects and pikas would have made the day complete, but he was nowhere in sight.

East South Fork Flathead—The north-central boundary of the Bob Marshall and western slopes of the Flathead Range are bounded by 57,640 roadless acres east of the South Fork Flathead and Hungry Horse Reservoir. Extensive limestone caves overlook the Spotted Bear River. Grizzlies rely upon these lower wildlands in the spring, as do migratory elk in winter.

Middle Fork Flathead—The northern edges of the Great Bear Wilderness overlooking the Middle Fork Flathead, Bear Creek, and up along the Continental Divide are augmented by 42,450 acres of roadless country. Bald eagles nest near the Middle Fork, goats work the steep faces of Slippery Bill Mountain, and grizzlies use these wild fringes to get from one place to another. Bull trout spawn in each of the major streams that flow south to the Middle Fork.

Badger-Two Medicine—The Rocky Mountain Front is the dramatic transition from mountains to prairie along an overpowering sweep of limestone scarps from Badger-Two Medicine south to Falls Creek-Silver King. The 120,000-acre Badger-Two Medicine wild area is strategically positioned between Glacier Park, the Great Bear and Bob Marshall wilderness areas, and the high plains of the Blackfeet Indian Reservation. The Badger is startling in its abrupt transition from rugged Continental Divide peaks to prairie, where moist maritime air makes it wetter and more diverse than the remainder of the front to the south. Further, it functions as a biological corridor between Glacier and the Bob Marshall Wilderness complex. East-flowing Badger Creek is guarded by steep massifs of limestone dissected by narrow canyons and waterways. The roughness of the country provides vital seclusion to reclusive grizzlies and gray wolves, along with protective cliffs for mountain goats. Wildlife increases in the more subdued South Fork Two Medicine drainage, with frequent signs of elk, deer, moose, sheep and black bear. One might flush a nesting Canada goose along a riparian meadow only to meet a grizzly around the next bend.

A resurgence in the practice of traditional Blackfeet religion depends on the pristine quality of the Badger-Two Medicine. The importance of the entire roadless area to traditional practice is best told by the Blackfeet. To nine-year-old Nah-too-ah-kee Okena Kipp, the Badger "...is the last place we have to practice our religion in an undisturbed manner—if they build roads the animals would not have a place to live."

Teton River High Peaks—From the Boone and Crockett Theodore Roosevelt Ranch south to unmistakable Ear Mountain, the 77,572-acre Teton roadless subregion includes foothill-prairie wildlands in the Blackleaf and Ear Mountain wildlife management areas, Bureau of Land Management's (BLM) Blind Horse Outstanding Natural Area, and The Nature Conservancy Pine Butte Preserve. Here in these remote fens and foothills, the plains grizzly makes its last stand on the continent. To the west, the Teton Peaks are the loftiest pinnacles on the front. Formed by thrust faults with steep east faces and gentle west slopes, these mountains are cut by a maze of valleys and streams. Both grizzlies and mountain goats are

JOHN REDDY

Above: *North Fork of the Sun River, Bob Marshall Wilderness Area.*

Facing page: *In the "Bob": top, Danaher Basin; bottom left, Badger Creek; right, Silvertip Peak.*

29

common on the Bob Marshall's highest point—massive 9,392' Rocky Mountain Peak. The country fills the senses with impressions of gleaming limestone, gnarled limber pine and wind, always the wind. If the wind lets up along the front it does so only briefly and then, it seems, only to gather more strength.

Deep Creek—The central winter range of the largest native herd of bighorn sheep in the lower 48 is within the 52,329-acre Deep Creek roadless area, which includes several BLM wild stretches of foothills and plains below the great slanting forms of Chute Mountain and Castle Reef. Westward, toward the crest of the Rocky Mountain Front range, a series of high parallel overthrust limestone reefs separate deep, sparsely forested valleys. Open south-facing gulches provide winter forage for migrating Sun River elk, mule deer, whitetails and as many as 1,000 bighorn sheep. The Forest Service study of wilderness attributes awarded Deep Creek a perfect score of 28, the highest such rating of any roadless area in the nation.

Renshaw—The 57,611-acre Renshaw roadless subregion is bounded by Gibson Reservoir on the north and the Benchmark road to the south. This diverse land is made up of three distinct landforms. Patrick's Basin drains north through a wide, heavily forested valley used by migrating Sun River elk. This area also may be the finest grizzly country on the front. Next, the high, grassy Fairview-Fork Creek plateau is a blend of winter and spring habitat for elk and bighorn sheep. The third area, the South Fork of the Sun, is the most popular east-side route to the Bob. The imposing east face of 8,246' Fairview Mountain is seen far out on the plains. Steep limestone reefs along the front give way to sharp peaks, forests and high mountain parks to the west that were converted to grasslands by fires during the 1920s.

Falls Creek-Silver King—The southernmost segment of the Rocky Mountain Front, south of Benchmark, is 75,417 acres of high peaks and steep canyons adjacent to the Scapegoat Wilderness, called Falls Creek-Silver King after a major drainage and mountain. The front range rises in majesty to the alpine summits of Crown and Steamboat mountains. Expansive Falls Creek is the largest unprotected pristine watershed on the Front south of Badger-Two Medicine. Grizzlies den and elk calve near the Continental Divide at the head of the East Fork of Falls Creek. The Divide itself is distinctly marked by wind-carved sandstone pedestals 20 to 50 feet high. Born on Scapegoat Mountain, the wild Dearborn River cuts a steep-walled gorge through Devil's Glen. Rapids alternate with deep emerald pools before the river flattens out into a wide rocky valley.

Stonewall Mountain—The southeast corner of the

JOHN REDDY

Scapegoat Wilderness is flanked by 51,537 acres of glacial headwalls and basins in the Stonewall Mountain roadless subregion. Historic Lewis and Clark Pass was crossed by Lewis on July 7, 1806 during the return journey. It also is the site of a prehistoric medicine wheel of embedded stones that point to the sun as it rises over the Great Divide. With the exception of rolling mountains in Alice Creek, the country is steep and filled with cliffs and avalanche chutes. The southeast slopes of the highest peak in the Bob Marshall country—9,411' Red Mountain—support a unique community of whitebark and limber pine growing together at 8,000'.

The southern reaches of the Bob Marshall Wilderness are buffered by the 104,100-acre Monture roadless area, which includes a small portion of the Clearwater Wildlife Management Area near Ovando Mountain. This includes the proposed Arnold Bolle Addition to the Scapegoat Wilderness. Two major drainages flow south to the Big Blackfoot through deep canyons and wide forested valleys—Monture Creek and the North Fork Blackfoot. The North Fork/Hobnail Tom Trail, named in honor of the late pioneer outfitter Tom Edwards, winds through miles of blackened trees, where the 1988 quarter-million-acre Canyon Creek fire reached its hottest intensity. In contrast, the long Monture Valley is covered with green forest from giant old-growth larch to gnarled whitebark pine at the head of open alpine amphitheaters. Cirque basins, tarn lakes and U-shaped valleys where grizzlies roam bear witness to past glaciation. Monture is also a major elk migration route between the Bob and the Clearwater winter range.

Swan Front/Swan Crest—The 272,320-acre roadless Swan Range is the formidable western guardian of the Bob, extending 100 miles from the Blackfoot Valley north to Badrock Canyon near Glacier's west entrance. The Swan Face is that southern two thirds of the range from the Clearwater-Swan Divide to Sixmile Mountain. A once-great sea left fossils along the top of the eastward-leaning Swans, which stand as mute testimony to awesome, ongoing land-carving forces.

From its austere, treeless crest to its foothold in the timbered Swan Valley 5,000 feet below, the Swan Face is an ecological whole with five major zones: high peaks and alpine basins; intermediate and hanging valleys; canyon country; ridge-valley faces; and the main Lion Creek Canyon.

The high peaks are epitomized by 9,356' Holland and 9,289' Swan, which are adorned with small but active glaciers. High basins along the crest are prime habitat for creatures from grizzlies to mountain goats to Clark's nutcrackers. Hanging valleys occur between the alpine zone and the fall line where streams plunge sharply into canyons. Pine martens, denizens of the boreal forest, depend upon pockets of old-growth spruce and fir in these intermediate basins. Canyon country extends from the lips of these basins to where streams leave the mountains. Ledges in these inaccessible narrow canyons are the best remaining niches for bobcat and lynx. The abrupt faces of the Swan contribute much to its inspirational value—that undefinable renewal of spirit gained by looking up at pristine mountains.

Lion Creek deserves special mention because it is the longest undisturbed drainage in the Swan. Wide hanging valleys are separated by cascades flowing over great barriers of rock. The largest hanging valleys host cathedral-like stands of ancient giant cedars. Above this untouched old growth, locked in by cliffs, are two major waterfalls with spellbinding power and height.

The spectacular Alpine Trail runs along the unbroken

Above: *Castle Reef, north of the Sun River, guards the Deep Creek portion of the Rocky Mountain Front.*

Facing page: *The wild Swans rise dramatically to the east of Holland Lake.*

BILL CUNNINGHAM

Above: Looking to Swan Peak from Swan Crest.
Right: Yellow columbine.

KRISTI DuBOIS

crest of the Swan to that northern sentinel of the range—7,234' Columbia Mountain. En route, it passes through magical Jewel Basin. The Jewel is a treasure of 28 sparkling alpine lakes surrounded by low rocky mountains with great vertical relief, bubbly streams, wet meadows and open-grown subalpine forest. With gentle east slopes, mountain goats favor the more rugged west side of the crest.

And so we complete our circle tour of the nearly 2½-million-acre Bob Marshall Wilderness country. Two roadless "orphans" are close to, but separated from, the main body of the Bob country. The Beaver-Willow road cuts off one of the most spectacular segments of the Rocky Mountain Front—the 20,500-acre Sawtooth roadless area, which includes the jagged "sawteeth" of Sawtooth Ridge on the Sun River Wildlife Management Area. This is truly up-and-down country where the land slants straight down to the creek bottoms. Limestone dominates the rough landscape with sheer cliffs, reefs, rubble and lofty pinnacles. One early spring evening while pitching camp at the head of Home Gulch, we were overwhelmed by views of Sawtooth, another huge basin to the south, and limestone slopes dotted with small bands of bighorn sheep and mule deer. North of Sawtooth, rolling hills and parks carpeted with aspen, grasslands and scattered clumps of limber pine and Douglas fir faded into the distance. That night the wind shook our tent like a giant hand. We awoke to see the splintered remains of a huge fir tree that had been snapped in two like a toothpick by the windstorm. The complete skeleton of a bighorn ram lay frozen into the ice of a creek next to camp. We wondered what had caused his fate. Winter kill? Mountain lion? Harsh and unforgiving is this Sawtooth country.

The 8,125-acre Lincoln Gulch roadless area is due south of the Scapegoat Wilderness next to the old Lincoln townsite. With steep, dense lodgepole pine thickets, this trailless enclave is among the town of Lincoln's favorite backyard elk-hunting spots. Broad, bare ridges run on both sides of Arrastra Creek, which cuts through the center of the roadless area below the exposed summit of 7,432' Black Mountain.

12 Mission Mountains Wilderness

The steeper slopes of the Mission Mountains on both sides of a jagged 40-mile crest remain wild. The Missions, both east and west, are one interdependent 174,377-acre wildland despite administration split between the Forest Service and Flathead Indian Reservation.

The east side of this long, lean north-south range con-

OUTFITTING IN THE WILDERNESS

Missoula-based outfitter Smoke Elser remembers when an outfitter's license sold for $10 over the counter. There was no limit on the number of horses or guests in the wilderness. A party might consist of 50 people and twice that many horses and mules. This was back in 1957, when Smoke began working for legendary pioneer outfitter Tom Edwards. Smoke credits "Hobnail" Tom with giving him the basic philosophy and ethics of operating in the wilderness, a philosophy that has made him a national standard-setter in light-on-the-land outfitting techniques. Above all, Smoke has heeded Tom's advise that "if you're going into the outfitting business you've got to give quality rather than quantity."

Smoke could see that large numbers of horses and people were doing a lot of damage, and that the guests were getting forced marches from one big impacted camp to another, instead of what they really wanted out of the wilderness.

By the time Smoke started his own outfit in the early 1960s, he was already practicing low-impact horse use, and has since evolved a no-impact ethic. A natural-born innovator, Smoke designs, makes and uses light-weight equipment that is durable, multi-functional and "works every time." His compact camp stove is a prime example of multi-purpose gear. It provides heat and cooking along with a removable top that allows the warmth of an open fire, sitting above ground without the scar of a fire ring. Up to four people can sleep and stand up in a seven-and-a-half-pound tipi. No one goes hungry on one of Smoke's trips, but food weight is cut in half by getting rid of the packaging. Less weight means less stock, which means less impact on the wilderness. A modest savings of only 20 pounds per mule reduces the number of pack animals by 10 percent. And the stock that Smoke ends up taking into the wilderness wear special flat shoes that leave light tracks similar to an unshod horse.

All this boils down to a standard of quality that doesn't come cheap. In order to ensure quality, Smoke goes on every trip, including 15 or more during the summer, two early fall photography tours in the Sun River Game Preserve, and four hunting trips in the Camp Pass area of the southern Bob Marshall Wilderness Area. He's in the saddle for more than 2,000 wilderness miles each season, camping out more than 100 nights from June to November. "I always start out counting the stars to fall asleep by; so far I've gotten up to nine," laughed Smoke.

When Smoke sets up camp he wants his guests to feel as though no one has ever been there before. He achieves this by being "the greatest robber in the world because I can steal the wilderness without ever getting caught by leaving no sign of our presence." Wide meadows with lots of horse feed don't measure up to the quality Smoke wants for his clients. His intimate knowledge of the Bob combined with no-trace camping and less stock allows him to take his guests off "the beaten track into higher-quality, more pristine wilderness.

After an eight-day trip in the wilds, Smoke's guests may be ready for a hot shower but "they'll never wash away the wilderness." Offering much more than a mere three-mile-per-hour transportation service, Smoke interprets what people are feeling and sensing, from the tiniest flower to the most awesome geologic formation.

The enterprising outfitter has turned a five-month season into a year-round business by teaching others his wilderness ethics and values. He spends three months in the spring at the Forest Service Wildlands Training Center at Ninemile instructing on horsemanship, packing skills and no-impact camping. Smoke helped screen 400 applicants for 55 positions at the center's first wilderness management training seminar held during May 1990.

The workshop helped solidify what many hope is a revitalized commitment to high-quality wilderness management within the agency.

Smoke is actively involved in the Bob Marshall Limits of Acceptable Change (LAC) process. To him, LAC is "like dough in a bread pan that I can mold. It's not set in concrete. We present ideas to the wilderness and if the wilderness says no we go back to the drawing board. The users change to fit the resource, not the other way around."

Smoke sees a parallel in the future of wilderness outfitting. The small, quality outfits that adjust to the wilderness resource will be the survivors. The philosophy of this survivor is summed up by the succinct message of a bumper sticker designed by his daughter, "This Family Sustained by Wilderness."

MICHAEL CRUMMETT

In the Strawberry Creek area of the Bob Marshall.

RICK & SUSIE GRAETZ

sists mostly of the 73,877-acre Mission Mountains Wilderness which is accessed by a maze of logging roads in the checkerboard-pattern ownership of Swan Valley. The Missions were formed from ancient Precambrian sedimentary rocks, which were then uplifted and tilted to the east. More recently, the upper layers of the Belt rock were washed away by the large-scale erosion of Ice Age glaciers, leaving today's striking mountainscape of rocky crags, sheer cliffs, knife ridges, cirques, horns, arêtes, U-shaped valleys and hundreds of tarns. Sparkling clear streams tumble over bedrock to the Swan Valley thousands of feet below. As with the west-side tribal Wilderness the most difficult terrain is in the southern Missions with elevational relief up to 5,000 feet.

Plant life varies from the deformed shapes of stunted trees along the Mission Divide to at least two rare species unique to these mountains. Limestone rock in combination with high altitude provides special habitat for tenacious yet fragile kittentails and bittercress.

Popularly known as the American Alps, the awesome western face of the Missions stabs the sky almost 7,000 vertical feet above the valley floor. In 1979 the Confederated Salish and Kootenai Tribes designated 89,500 acres of privately-owned tribal lands along the western slopes as Wilderness—the first such wildland dedication by any tribe on its own. Although their declaration was patterned to some extent after the 1964 Wilderness Act, the common theme of management demonstrates the tribe's own cultural and spiritual links to wilderness.

The Missions' apex is atop the glacier-studded majesty of 9,820' McDonald Peak in the rugged south end, where a dozen other pinnacles rise above 9,000'. Perpetual snowfields feed hundreds of gem-like tarns in one of the densest concentrations of alpine lakes in the northern Rockies. Waterfalls are abundant, with the best-known being the 1,000-foot plunges of Elizabeth and Mission falls.

The tribal Wilderness is managed with a special priority for wildlife. Each summer a dozen or more grizzlies gather on the snowfields of McDonald Peak to feast on swarms of cutworm moths and ladybugs. In order to avoid displacing these great bears, the tribe has closed about 12,000 acres to all public use from mid-July to October. The closed area is part of a larger trailless region that serves to discourage humans from entering critical grizzly habitat.

To some, the Missions are a pint-sized Glacier Park. To others their special feature is the profusion of water, in all its forms, seemingly everywhere. In the words of the tribe's Save the Mission Mountains Committee: "These mountains belong to our children, and when our children grow old they will belong to their children. In this way and for this reason these mountains are sacred."

13 Wild Horse Island

During the first half of the 19th century, Blackfeet periodically entered the Flathead Valley to steal horses from the Flatheads, who therefore hid their horses on a large, mountainous island in a big lake—2,165-acre Wild Horse Island in Flathead Lake. Descendents of these Indian ponies may have survived into the 1980s, but today "Wild Horse" exists in name only. It is the lake's prominent landmark, a mostly wild mound rising a half mile from the west shore. Despite 17 private cabins dotting its shoreline, at least 2,100 acres remain wild, with the mute remains of old buildings telling of failed homesteads from 1910 to 1915.

The north- and east-facing slopes support a heavy mix of stately ponderosa pine, Douglas fir, aspen, cottonwoods, mosses and ferns. In the spring, bare grassy hills are ablaze with yellow balsamroot and pink bitterroots.

Forests, rocky cliffs, grasslands, natural salt licks and surrounding fresh water add up to a self-contained habitat for mule deer, coyote, osprey, hawk and bald eagle. But Wild Horse is most renowned for its bighorn sheep, which are easily viewed during most hikes there. The most spectacular walk heads east up the main ridge to Eye Glass Peak, highest point on the island. Wild Horse Island State Park is managed for day use only, to protect a delicate balance within its microcosm of wildland and wildlife.

Total wildlands in Glacier/Bob Marshall Country: 3,958,310 acres
Total designated Wilderness in region: 1,698,729 acres (42.9%)

LARRY MAYER

Above: Wild Horse Island.

Facing page: The Rocky Mountain Front near Pine Butte.

GARY D. HOLMES

THE GREAT BOB TREK: AROUND THE BOB IN 60 DAYS

The clouds opened to sunshine on that mid-June, 1987 morning, as 40 people gathered at the Aspen Grove Campground seven miles east of Lincoln to officially dedicate the start of a 60-day, 350-mile odyssey—the Great Bob Trek. Beginning on the southeast edge of the 2½-million-acre Bob Marshall Wilderness Country at historic Lewis and Clark Pass, the trekkers planned to encircle the Bob by hiking through the proposed peripheral additions to the Bob Marshall Wilderness.

The ceremony began with several songs, notably "Forever Wild," by legendary Montana hiker/musician Walkin' Jim Stoltz.

Walkin' Jim was also the trip leader for the monumental trek. Montana Wilderness Association program director John Gatchell expressed the hope that the trek would "increase public awareness of that which is vulnerable by working through the unprotected areas."

Noted wildlife conservationist Jim Posewitz recalled the many whose lives have been "invested in this wildland. This Great Trek is the people's expression—it is the people crying out for this wildland." Jim harkened back to the days when the land to the north was ravaged and depleted. "Now the land is great because it is a wild community which the people have restored—a symphony forever unfinished, with each generation adding a new chorus." Jim gave credit to the Forest Service for establishing the initial protection for much of the Bob Marshall Country, "but both Bob Marshall and Aldo Leopold of the Forest Service knew that there had to be a popular movement for wilderness." How fitting, he observed, that the trek was beginning on the edge of the Scapegoat Wilderness, which in 1972 became the nation's first de facto wilderness to be added to the Wilderness system—a great battle fought and won through citizen initiative.

On August 9, Bob Marshall's birthday was celebrated along the high Swan Divide just south of Inspiration Pass. Elaine Snyder baked a birthday cake in memory of Bob. The cake was quickly devoured, along with a bottle of good wine, by 30 celebrants. Walkin' Jim sang a song that he had just composed in the wilds, which was inspired by Norman Mclean's wonderful book, *A River Runs Through It*. A core threesome had trekked the entire 350 miles to this point from Lewis and Clark Pass—Mickey Smith, Karen Maas and Walkin' Jim. Others had joined and left along the way. Elaine read from writings of Bob Marshall, and John Gatchell shared excerpts from Bud Moore's journal. Karen told us about the wild Swans. "It only gets better," she said. At times, the group felt as though it was on the mountaintop with Julie Andrews in "The Sound of Music."

Bob Marshall Alliance chairman Jim Curtis, his daughter and two young grandchildren along with a pair of trusty burros, led the trekkers down the Gorge Creek trail that evening. For the next week they paralleled the crest of the Swans en route to the conclusion of the trek at Holland Lake on August 15.

And what a grand celebration it was, as veteran Montana conservationist and woodsman Bud Moore spoke to a festive gathering of more than 200, thanking the trekkers for a "job well done." Bud told of what the Wilderness means to those in the Swan Valley: "We're fortunate, in that we can go in either direction, east or west, and the farther we go the wilder the country becomes. For those of us who live and work here, wilderness shapes our economy and culture and what we are as a community. What we do with our wildlands has much to do with what we are. If we disposed of our wild country we'd be lesser people."

Walkin' Jim deepened the euphoria with his new composition, "River Runnin' Through It." He explained how he usually writes a new song every 100 miles on the trail. "This summer I came up with only one in about 400 miles, but I think it's a good one. The river that flows through all of us linking us to the wildlands."

BILL CUNNINGHAM

Above: Montana minstrel Walkin' Jim Stoltz leading the Great Bob Trek.

Facing page: Middle Fork of the Flathead in the Bob.

37

WILDLAND AND WILDFIRE

It had been a tough grunt to 7,400' Limestone Pass on the southern edge of the Bob Marshall Wilderness that late July day, but the toe-jamming seven-mile descent to the Danaher was even harder on our guided backpacking party. Our dream of a mellow cruise into the remote Danaher Basin by way of the gentle North Fork Blackfoot/Dry Fork route was dashed by the Canyon Creek fire of 1988. Looking east across the Continental Divide we could see the flame-reddened base of a 25,000' mushroom cloud of smoke billowing from the then-22,000-acre Scapegoat Wilderness fire.

A month earlier I had accompanied outfitter Smoke Elser and a group of 10 on a four-day horse packing trip through the Scapegoat. June 25, 1988, had been hot and sultry. Each of us thought about fire danger as we rode through tinder-dry brush. Late afternoon brought huge anvil-shaped thunderheads; the air thickened with the mounting tension of an impending storm. By late evening our camp at the mouth of Canyon Creek was enveloped by dark clouds, thunder and flashes of lightning. Suddenly, we saw a vertical bolt of lightning strike the rocky spine of a small ridge a quarter mile above camp, instantly erupting into a ball of fire! The strike was immediately followed by sheets of driving rain, leading us to believe that the fire would be short-lived. Not so. An hour after the first spark we found the smoking fire burning a pocket of snags on a steep slope covered with thick forest litter. Despite heavy all-night rainfall, the tenacious little one-third-acre fire was red hot the next morning. It had started next to an eerie, seemingly bottomless cavern of black water local outfitters call "The Devil's Bathtub." Had Satan called the lightning down to heat his bathwater? we asked, only half joking.

The strike we had witnessed started the Canyon Creek fire in a Wilderness with an approved fire management plan, so the Lolo National Forest managers decided to let it burn naturally under prescribed conditions. "Watch it, but let it burn," crackled the reply over the radio when the fledgling Canyon Creek fire was reported by the wilderness guard on the morning of June 26. The smoldering hot spot was confined by rocks on three sides. Certainly no one would have predicted that July and August would bring extreme winds with no moisture.

The fire remained inactive for a month until July 21 when high winds blew it up to 2,000 acres. During our late July hike into the Bob the flames moved into East Fork Creek, settling down until August 9 when they expanded to 33,000 acres. On August 29, powerful winds pushed the fire several miles outside the Wilderness boundary, raising it to 55,000 acres. The most dramatic movement occurred on September 6, when extreme wind patterns caused the fire to erupt overnight to 180,000 acres. Finally, on September 10, the inferno was knocked down by rain and snow, stopping at a burned perimeter of 240,600 acres. Although large blocks of unburned islands were scattered throughout, the fire still charred more than half the Scapegoat Wilderness making it the largest naturally-ignited fire within a designated Wilderness since the inception of the Forest Service natural-fire policy.

How ironic, I thought, wiping the sweat from my brow, that a fire I could have put out a month ago is causing us to huff and puff over a much tougher route to and from the Danaher. What the heck, it's a small price to pay for a long overdue moderation of the once knee-jerk practice of putting out all wildfires.

Later that fall as I wandered through a mosaic of blackened and unburned forest I was delighted to discover the process of recovery. Everywhere, it seemed, was the vibrant green of new grasses and the re-sprouting of fire-tolerant shrubs, such as chokecherry. In the mountains of Montana natural vegetation has evolved with climate and fire as driving forces. Fire is part of a complex interaction of ecological processes that act upon the ecosystem. If we are to preserve wild forests we also must preserve the processes through which these forests evolve. While every effort must be made to prevent the kind of damage to private property caused by the Canyon Creek fire, it is also true that periodic large fires within Wilderness are both necessary and inevitable.

In many areas, the past 70 years of fire suppression has caused an unnatural heavy buildup of forest fuel. It's not surprising that giant wildfires, like Canyon Creek, burn more destructively than they otherwise would were it not for our interruption of natural fire frequencies. The life cycles of some trees, like lodgepole and ponderosa pine, de-

BILL CUNNINGHAM

Smoke Elser on the Canyon Creek Fire, June 1988.

pend upon fire. Many lodgepole cones will not release their seeds unless they are opened by the heat of a hot fire. The thick bark of mature ponderosa allows it to withstand surface fire. As the surrounding vegetation burns off, young trees can better compete for water and nutrients.

Then there is the question of global warming, spurred at an unprecedented rate by an alarming increase in carbon dioxide. The effects of global warming will change the frequency, severity and timing of fire. For example, after enough time to achieve equilibrium following an average yearly increase of 5 degrees centigrade, vegetation zones would shift about 900 meters up the mountainside or 500 kilometers northward.

Will wilderness remain "untrammeled" in a human-induced planetary climate change? As one researcher put it, the question may no longer be what are the limits of acceptable change, but how do we manage inevitable change?

FIRES & WHITEBARK PINE

The red squirrel scolded to no avail as the huge grizzly dug into the squirrel's hard-earned cache of nutritious whitebark pine nuts below a windswept ridge near timberline. Winter was coming early to the high country and the great bear knew that he would need all the large, high-energy nuts he could find before hibernation.

To many, this scene symbolizes wilderness, particularly since "wilderness on the rocks" high mountain ecosystems make up so much of the Wilderness system. At the same time, these ecosystems are undergoing dramatic, long-lasting changes because the circle of fire, birds and whitebark pine has been broken. Concern focuses on the hardy whitebark pine, which grows slowly in the highest of forests and at timberline. In western Montana whitebark pine is declining so fast that the tree may not be able to regenerate itself.

Oil-rich whitebark pine seeds are the favored food of Clark's nutcrackers, which in turn disperse the seeds for regeneration. After filling their specially adapted pouches with up to 150 ripening seeds during late summer forays, the birds bury a few at a time in exposed sites, sometimes up to 14 miles from seed sources. The birds never recover many seeds, so whitebark pine gets started on remote alpine ridges and in large burns.

With its distinctive upswept branches and twisted shapes, whitebark pine epitomizes the alpine, and it feeds nutcrackers, squirrels and bears. Its vital importance to aesthetics and wildlife underscores rising concern over a shocking decline—90 percent of the whitebark pine on the east slopes of Glacier National Park are dead or dying. In the North Fork Wildlands of the Whitefish Range as many as two thirds of the trees have been lost in the last decade.

White pine blister rust, mountain pine beetle epidemics, and fire suppression are to blame. Introduced from Europe, the blister rust disease is extensive in the wetter mountain country of northwest Montana. The spores of the rust do not spread as rapidly in drier regions, such as Greater Yellowstone.

Fire suppression since the early 1900s has resulted in vast forests of old lodgepole pine vulnerable to severe mountain pine beetle epidemics. The infestations spread upward to whitebark pine from lower-elevation lodgepole forests.

Periodic ground fires help propagate the more fire-resistant whitebark pine individuals by killing their competitor, subalpine fir, and making small openings where whitebark pine can reproduce. Severe fires also are helpful by enabling whitebark pine to sprout from birds' caches in the exposed mineral soils of burns. With fire suppression, whitebark pine stands age and become more susceptible to insects, disease, and competition from spruce and fir in subalpine forests.

Allowing some natural fires to burn in wilderness is positive but only part of the solution, according to Forest Service scientist Steve Arno. If whitebark pine is to survive its triple threat of insects, disease and longer fire intervals, more research is needed to learn how to apply prescribed fire for the benefit of the species. Breaking the circle of fire, seed dispersal by Clark's nutcrackers and renewal of whitebark pine threatens Montana's alpine wilderness, including the very existence of the great bear as he prepares for his long winter sleep.

BILL CUNNINGHAM

Whitebark forest at 9,000' elevation in the West Big Hole.

THE UPPER CLARK FORK

LEFT: RONALD J. GLOVAN; BELOW: ERWIN & PEGGY BAUER; RIGHT: BILL CUNNINGHAM

The Upper Clark Fork is Montana's heartland, just as wild country survives in the heart of the region's varied mountain ranges. From the Continental Divide to the Garnets to the Flint Creeks to the Sapphires to the Rattlesnakes, wildlands are almost always in view of local folks—whether they live in town or in the country.

Above: Cottonwood Meadows, Hoodoo Wilderness Study Area.
Left: Bobcat and prey.
Far left: Mt. Powell and Elliot Lakes, Flint Creek Range.

41

THE UPPER CLARK FORK

Physiographic region COMPLEX Area Name	Area No.†	Montana Gross Acreage	Agency/ Ownership	Management Status
III. Upper Clark Fork				
UPPER BLACKFOOT/GREAT DIVIDE	14			
Anaconda Hill		17,709	FS	R-NW
Specimen Creek		17,709	FS	R-NW
Crater Mtn.		9,291	FS	R-NW
Nevada Mtn.		49,939	FS	R-NW
Electric Peak		47,005	FS	R-NW
OGDEN MTN.	15	12,218	FS	R-NW
GARNET RANGE	16			
Wales Creek		11,580	BLM	BLM WSA
Hoodoo Mtn.		15,637	BLM	BLM WSA, R-NW
FLINT CREEK RANGE	17			
Flint Creek/Dolus		60,297	FS	R-NW
Fred Burr		6,643	FS	R-NW
SILVER KING	18	65,767	FS	R-NW
SOUTHERN SAPPHIRE FLANKS	19			
Tolan Creek		7,128	FS	R-NW
Sleeping Child		22,243	FS	R-NW
Emerine		16,161	FS	R-NW
NORTHERN SAPPHIRES	20			
Stony Mtn.		103,346	FS	R-NW
Quigg		82,505	FS	R-NW, BLM WSA
Welcome Creek Wilderness		29,235	FS	W, R-NW
RATTLESNAKE WILDERNESS & NRA	21			
Rattlesnake Wilderness		32,844	FS	W
Rattlesnake NRA		22,000	FS	NRA
Contiguous lands		10,156	FS	R-NW
South Fork Primitive Area		36,000	T	TPA
(Contiguous Rattlesnake/South Fork Wildlands: 101,000 acres)				
PETTY MTN./DEEP CREEK	22			
Petty Mtn.		16,980	FS	R-NW
Deep Creek		8,170	FS	R-NW
NATIONAL BISON RANGE	23	8,000	FWS	NWR
NINEMILE/RESERVATION DIVIDE	24			
Reservation Divide		16,300	FS	R-NW
Flathead Resservation Divide		15,000	T	
Stark Mtn.		14,140	FS	R-NW
NORTH & SOUTH SIEGEL	25			
North Siegel		10,200	FS	R-NW
South Seigel		15,600	FS	R-NW

Total Wildlands: 779,803 acres. Wilderness: 60,979 acres (7.8%).

†For identification purposes in this book only
*Areas with contiguous wildlands in Idaho
**Areas with contiguous wildlands in Wyoming

KEY
Agency Symbols
BLM—Bureau of Land Management
FS—Forest Service
FWS—Fish & Wildlife Service
MDFWP—Montana Dept. of Fish, Wildlife & Parks
NPS—National Park Service
P—Private
S—State
SEA—USDA Science & Education Administration
T—Tribal
TNC—The Nature Conservancy

Management Status Symbols
ACEC—BLM Area of Critical Environmental Concern
BLM WSA—Bureau of Land Management Wilderness Study Area
FPA—Forest Service Further Planning Area
ISA—Instant BLM Study Area
NP—National Park
NRA—National Recreation Area
NWR—National Wildlife Refuge
ONA—BLM Outstanding Natural Area
PP—Private Preserve
R-NW—Roadless-Nonwilderness
RWMA—Recreation & Wildlife Management Area
SP—State Park
TPA—Tribal Primitive Area
TR—Tribal Reserve

14 Upper Blackfoot/ Great Divide Wildlands

From Electric Peak northward along the Continental Divide there exists a string of wildlands at the source of the Big Blackfoot and Little Blackfoot rivers.

The Great Divide winds for 13 miles through the southern portion of the 47,005-acre wildlife-rich Electric Peak/ Little Blackfoot roadless, area reaching its apex at 8,597' Thunderbolt Mountain. To the immediate south a lush, mile-long meadow and lodgepole pine/spruce forest encircle Cottonwood Lake—a favored watering hole for summering elk, deer and moose. Over the Divide extensive beaver ponds in picturesque Blackfoot Meadows occupy most of a wide basin at the head of the Little Blackfoot River.

This "land of a thousand springs" is ideally suited for family excursions, a place where a youngster is likely to see a moose feeding in one pond while he himself is catching pan-sized cutthroat and brookies from another.

To the north between Helena and Lincoln, the 49,939-acre Nevada Mountain roadless area straddles the divide for 15 miles. The more prominent features are Nevada Mountain and Black Mountain—each rising above 8,000'. The heads of drainages along the Divide are characterized by scenic rocky cirques, particularly on the east side. On the west side, steep, densely-forested finger ridges are dotted with numerous grassy parks on the south-facing slopes. This mix of habitat is perfect for some 1,500 head of elk and nearly as many deer. Heavy roading and logging on all sides make the area's thick stands of lodgepole pine all the more important as elk security cover during hunting season. Because of deep snowpack and the numerous streams that head up along the Divide, Nevada Mountain is a large producer of pure water for downstream users in the Little Prickly Pear Creek and Blackfoot River drainages.

North of Stemple Pass, the Continental Divide touches the eastern edge of the 9,291-acre Crater Mountain roadless area, which has the Blackfoot River as its northern boundary. Between the Great Divide and the Big Blackfoot a series of small drainages separated by high, broad ridges flow westward. Grassy meadows are scattered throughout open Douglas fir and thick forests of old-growth lodgepole pine at higher elevations, where elk, deer and black bear are common. Crater Mountain at 7,128' is a popular destination of cross-country skiers and may also be a peregrine falcon nesting site.

The Great Divide changes to a broad, flat 7,000' ridge as it trends northeast through the center of the 17,709-acre Specimen Creek roadless area toward Flesher Pass. Small streams and lodgepole pine-covered hillsides fall from both sides of the divide. The rough terrain provides hiding cover for elk as well as summer range and some winter habitat on drier Douglas-fir slopes at lower elevations.

The Anaconda Hill roadless area, equal in size to Specimen Creek, begins at Flesher Pass, overlapping the slopes of the Continental Divide for 13 miles to Rogers Pass on Highway 200. Both sides are characterized by sparse clumps of Douglas fir and lodgepole pine, with steep, open grassy sidehills, and fingers of small, splintered rock. The high, windy divide is a mosaic of fescue grassland and limber pine, lending itself to cross-country travel. In places the east side is abrupt with sheer rock faces rising several hundred feet. In the north end, near Midnight Hill, a visitor can savor the dramatic transition from mountain to prairie eastward as well as the vast wildland of Scapegoat Wilderness to the north.

15 Ogden Mountain

One of Lincoln's favorite backdoor walk-in places for big game hunting, especially during the early archery season, is the 12,218-acre Ogden Mountain roadless area. The mostly rolling terrain is broken up with flat, broad ridgetops and gradual sideslopes that become extremely steep in some of the larger drainages. A 100-acre boulder field hidden in the roadless core is unusual for the country around Lincoln. Seeps and springs abound, adding diversity and productivity for most wildlife species found in western Montana.

16 Garnet Range Wildlands

The 11,580 acres of Bureau of Land Management (BLM) roadless lands in the Wales Creek Wilderness Study Area (WSA) encompass the last major unroaded drainages in the heavily logged western Garnet Range. Upper Wales Creek is fed by numerous winding side drainages with dense forests of lodgepole pine, spruce, Douglas fir, larch, subalpine fir and aspen. A herd of 25 to 30

CHARLES E. KAY

Looking east from Mt. Powell to Mt. Deerlodge in the Flint Creek Mountains.

43

JOHN REDDY

moose thrive at beaver ponds and in wet meadows along the stream course. Besides being a native cutthroat fishery, Wales Creek contains at least four hot springs. Used by early miners, these thermal springs now attract skiers, hunters and other visitors to their warm waters.

Over the ridge to the south the Yourname Creek drainage is thickly timbered with lodgepole pine that provides needed security for elk in the fall. The uncut forests are also used for nesting by goshawks, a Montana species of special concern. A scramble up 6,860' Chamberlain Mountain yields a birdseye panorama of an unroaded expanse to the south. Ample solitude exists in these remote Blackfoot River tributaries.

The eastern Garnets contain two vestiges of wild country, administered by BLM and separated by a low-standard ridge road. As such, the 11,380-acre Hoodoo Mountain Wilderness Study Area (WSA) and the 4,257-acre Gallagher Creek WSA are considered here as a unified 15,637-acre wildland.

At 6,700', the spacious and lofty Cottonwood Meadows in the southeast corner is a distinctive landmark from which Wet Cottonwood Creek is born. Cliffs and talus rock tower above spongy meadows for miles down the drainage. Wet Cottonwood divides the area in half, with dense lodgepole pine, grassy parks and tiny creeks to the south around 7,438' Devil Mountain and north toward Hoodoo Mountain. Several marked foot trails made by sheepherders a half century ago are mostly used today by elk, deer and black bear.

The pristine headwaters of secluded Gallagher Creek begin just over the divide west of Cottonwood Meadows. Wild residents range from raptors in rugged cliffs at the head of the drainage to native cutthroat in shady pools, with elk sure to be close by. A visitor may stumble across pieces of petrified wood along the stream.

17 Flint Creek Range Wildlands

The 60,297-acre Flint Range/Dolus Lakes area comprises the roadless heart of the Flint Creek Range. Once divided by the low-standard Rock Creek Road, the country has been joined together by county abandonment of this jeep trail. All the major peaks in the range are within the roadless area, including Mt. Powell, loftiest point at 10,164'.

Still, the mountains here are lower, generally from 8,000' to 9,000', and more gently rounded than in other nearby ranges. Dozens of dark-colored alpine lakes lure walk-in anglers.

Near the perimeter, rolling hills covered with dense lodgepole pine and mixed conifers change abruptly to steep slopes with an array of trees, grass and rock talus. Upslope, the glaciated U-shaped canyons end in huge cirques with cliff faces crowned by blunt summits. Wind-twisted subalpine fir and whitebark pine are found at upper timberline. The highest ridges are punctuated with house-size boulders, often cloaked in black, yellow and orange lichens. Long, rounded grassy ridges radiate from the peaks, their sides falling sharply into tight avalanche chutes. From the Deer Lodge Valley, the long bare ridge between Deer Lodge Mountain and Mt. Powell looks level and rounded, but the entire back side is a sheer curving cliff called the "Crater."

The southwest corner of the Flints is occupied by the 6,643-acre Fred Burr roadless area, which is bounded on the south by the Discovery Basin Ski Area. This is rough country, made even more so by dense forest, heavy downfall and rocky hillsides that angle steeply about a half mile inside the boundary. Five major peaks with a variety of mountain top formations form the center of Fred Burr. Here a large, round cirque basin carved between two pinnacles leads to a saddle with a marshy meadow. Mountain goats find refuge on cliffs to the north.

18 Silver King

With the northern end split off by the BPA 500-kilovolt powerline, the 65,767-acre Silver King roadless area in the southern John Long Mountains is still a substantial wildland. This is high ridge country with a lightly-used main ridge trail winding north through open-growing whitebark pine for 15 miles from Black Pine Lookout past 7,581' Silver King to McDermott Creek. The divide is actually the eastern half of an elongated horseshoe-shaped ridge system surrounding a long U-shaped tributary to Rock Creek. The east-facing slopes are densely covered with lodgepole pine, Douglas fir and heavy downfall. The west slope cover is mixed, with clumps of Douglas fir and grassy parks.

19 Southern Flanks of the Sapphires

The 7,128-acre Tolan Creek unroaded area along the southwest edge of the Sapphire Range includes only the mid-segment of Tolan Creek. The upper reaches are developed by roads and timber harvest. Steep V-shaped drainages are separated by broad, rolling ridgetops. Ponderosa pine grows on south slopes and lower elevations, with Douglas fir at midslope and a mix of lodgepole pine and subalpine fir with beargrass understory high along the Continental Divide, which forms the southern boundary. Scars on large ponderosas bear witness to historical Native American use.

In 1961, the huge Sleeping Child Fire burned into the southeast corner of the 22,243-acre Sleeping Child roadless area in the southwest Sapphires. Like Tolan Creek, this wildland contains only the middle portion of its namesake drainage with forest development in the headwaters. Breaklands fall steeply into major streams contrasting with gently rolling terrain around the wet meadows of Barnett, Coyote and Two Bear on the east end. Occasional rock outcrops break up an otherwise continuous forest of lodgepole pine and Douglas fir that provides needed escape cover for elk in the fall.

As one of the highest peaks in the Sapphires, 8,639' Mt. Emerine rises in the heart of the 16,161-acre southeast Sapphires roadless area that bears its name. Emerine Ridge is a dominant feature in these upper Rock Creek headwaters, where Douglas fir grades into dense stands of lodgepole pine/subalpine fir and whitebark pine along the ridges. Massive granite boulders up to 10 feet in diameter are stacked along the divide like poker chips.

20 Northern Sapphires

North of Skalkaho Pass, three major wildlands grace the Sapphires, the first being the misnamed 103,346-acre Stony Mountain roadless area. In truth, there is no "Stony Mountain" within or anywhere near the boundary. Angular rock piles and gnarled whitebark pine define the 18 miles of Sapphire Mountain crest, which bisects this diverse landscape. The divide rises to aptly named 8,656' Dome Shaped Mountain, where cirques give evidence of past glaciation. The geology is complex with granitic intrusions, limestone, numerous faults and glacial deposits in the Upper Burnt Fork.

A vast forest of Douglas fir and lodgepole pine opens with several large natural meadows, five small lakes and countless potholes dotting the Skalkaho Basin near the south boundary. Most of the northern half is rocky, especially where breaklands plummet to the bigger streams. The exception is 10,000 acres of gently rolling lodgepole pine in the drainages that flow northeast into Rock Creek.

On the Bitterroot side of the divide Stony Mountain contains the 25,000-acre Skalkaho Game Preserve where visitors can observe and photograph elk, goats and other wildlife in the best summer/fall habitat in the Sapphires. The Palisade Mountain and Easthouse national recreation trails lead to several fishable lakes. Another trail serves Fuse Lake, which contains Arctic grayling.

Sliderock: tens of thousands of acres of it are scattered across half of the oval 82,505-acre Quigg roadless area. Immediately east of Stony Mountain, talus slopes and Douglas fir/lodgepole pine forests begin at Rock Creek and rise 4,500 feet to a series of high, open ridges and glacial moraines. The country is rugged enough for bighorn sheep and a few mountain goats, yet gentle enough for nursing and summering elk.

An entry from my journal describes a route from the summit of 8,419' Quigg Peak as "a classic descent from the top of a grassy, rock-strewn peak to a high, narrow ridge timbered with whitebark pine to a steep, open headwall to a lateral moraine above the creek and finally along a tight streambottom dropping several thousand feet with moss-covered boulders and a soft dirt trail underfoot."

ED TYANICH

Above: Lewis and Clark Pass from near Silver King Mountain.

Facing page: Blackfoot River.

BILL CUNNINGHAM

Rattlesnake National Recreation Area viewed from Stuart Peak.

21 Rattlesnake Mountains Wilderness Complex

Only four miles north of Missoula, the 61,000 acres of glaciated topography in the Rattlesnake Wilderness and National Recreation Area form Montana's premier urban Wilderness, blending the best of both wilderness and civilization. The U-shaped Rattlesnake basin is fed by more than 50 small creeks that begin as seeps from springs and melting snowbanks in the upper 32,844-acre Wilderness portion of the National Recreation Area. Resting in more than 30 mountain lakes, the icy water then plunges down waterfalls and steep-gradient streams. Each hanging valley is separated by sheer headwalls and forests of subalpine fir, lodgepole pine and spruce sloping down to open-grown Douglas fir and ponderosa pine parklands.

The nonwilderness part of the NRA, dedicated to wildlife and recreation, is guarded by the southern flanks of Stuart Peak. From this point north a knife ridge climbs still higher to the northern sentinel of the Rattlesnake—remote 8,620' McLeod Peak. The east side of the ridge is marked by cliffs, cirques and rolling basins of scattered subalpine forest where transplanted mountain goats are staging a comeback. The gentler western slopes lead down to the spacious bowl-like basin of upper Grant Creek. Although uncommon, grizzly bears roam these secluded wildlands, and once in a while the haunting howl of a lone wolf adds to the mystique.

The adjacent wildlands north of McLeod Peak and the rugged Rattlesnake Divide were once a vision-quest site for the Salish Indians. Today, the Flathead Indian Reservation protects this land—the South Fork Jocko Tribal Primitive Area—as a sacred place open only to tribal members. Thus, the remote upper Rattlesnake is made even more inaccessible from the north.

The Rattlesnake Range contains approximately 101,000 acres of contiguous wildlands standing as a lasting model of community determination to reclaim wildness from past logging, water development and intermingled private land. Retired University of Montana forestry dean Arnold Bolle describes this place as "…a pearl full of intimate little surprises…full of memories of happy kids, beautiful scenes, and special discoveries."

22 Petty Mountain/Deep Creek

A stable population of about 75 bighorn sheep resides along the rocky west face and high open parks of the 16,980-acre Petty Mountain roadless area 17

On the west side of Rock Creek directly northwest of Quigg sits the 28,135-acre Welcome Creek Wilderness, along with 1,100 acres of contiguous roadless land on its southern tip. The forested slopes, exposed ridges and deep canyons of this heart-shaped wildland contribute a rare example of lower-elevation general forest to the National Wilderness System. The land eases gently from the Sapphire Divide and then drops suddenly to form breaks that are surprisingly steep and rough. Old-growth stands of lodgepole pine mixed with sylvan groves of Douglas fir and spruce provide a home for pine marten, bobcat, raccoon, mink and weasel.

The wildness of Welcome Creek can be felt by reading from the October 14, 1974 journal of noted Montana conservationist Bud Moore: "Except for [Welcome] Creek's energetic music, I hiked alone in silence deepened by the mountain's shadow. Each intimate twist in the trail—there are many—opened sudden new vistas, mini worlds they were, each different from the last, expanding ahead then closing behind a giant rock point or spruce tree as I ambled on through the spell of evening hush."

miles west of Missoula. Timbered, rocky ridges feed in a circular patter into the rounded, grassy summit of 7,265' Petty Mountain, which rises 4,000 feet from Petty Creek in only two miles. Open south-facing savannahs attract summering elk and deer.

East of the Telephone Butte-Wildhorse Point Ridge is the 8,170-acre Deep Creek roadless area on the low, broad basin of Deep Creek. This rolling terrain is almost completely covered with a mixture of Douglas fir, lodgepole pine, larch and huckleberry.

23 National Bison Range

The National Bison Range in the Flathead Valley near Moiese was established in 1908 to protect one of the most significant of the remaining herds of American bison, or buffalo, where a population of 300 to 500 of the huge shaggy beasts roam over nearly 19,000 acres of grasslands. Introduced antelope, mule deer, whitetail deer, elk, bighorn sheep and mountain goats live together in a near-natural association, along with coyotes, bobcat and a few black bears. Centrally located Red Sheep Mountain is connected to the Mission Range by a descending spur and is actually an ancient island that was surrounded by Glacial Lake Missoula 12,000 to 14,000 years ago.

From the top of the 19-mile Red Sheep Mountain scenic drive near 4,885' Highpoint, approximately 8,000 acres of the most undeveloped land in the Bison Range extends downhill to the south and west, interrupted only by a few fences and low-standard service roads. Visitors along the scenic drive are restricted from the open range except under special permit.

Rolling slopes of native Palouse prairie are interspersed with stringers of Douglas fir on north-facing aspects and ponderosa pine on warmer southern exposures. Swales and rocky outcrops give rise to snowberry, serviceberry, rose and other browse.

24 Ninemile/Reservation Divides

The 14,140-acre Stark Mountain unroaded area, named after a 7,340' pinnacle with an active lookout, straddles about eight miles of the divide between the Ninemile Valley and the Clark Fork. The divide displays small cirque basins topped with whitebark pine and a small amount of mountain hemlock. Narrow forested valleys separated by sharp ridges feed into Ninemile, with gentler topography and rocky ridges dropping to the Clark Fork side. Legend has it that an old Indian burial ground is hidden here.

Across the valley to the north, the Reservation Divide forms the rugged backbone between Ninemile and the Flathead Indian Reservation. Along its crest, a roadless area of about 31,300 acres drapes both sides to about mid-slope. From the distinctive, cone-shaped summit of 7,996' Squaw Peak—highest point on the divide—this wildland extends northwest for 30 twisting, up and down miles.

Scree slopes near the crest plummet to the more gradual headwall basins of major streams. On the reservation side below secluded Three Lakes Peak, slight glaciation has formed hanging valleys and partial cirques notched into several north-facing peaks holding small, deep lakes. Although close to the populated Ninemile Valley, the country is still wild enough for an occasional wolf, attracted no doubt by a large whitetail deer prey base. Giant western redcedar and devil's club understory in Kennedy Creek make yet another surprise in this "backdoor" wildland.

25 North and South Siegel

The North and South Siegel roadless areas are just beyond Siegel Pass at the northwest tip of Reservation Divide. Horseshoe-shaped North Siegel consists of 10,200 unroaded acres wrapped around the northwest-southeast ridgeline of Siegel Peak. Steep, narrow valleys with rock ledges and scattered Douglas fir, larch and ponderosa pine drain to the Clark Fork and Flathead rivers.

To the west the narrow north-facing slopes of the Ninemile-Keystone Divide in the 15,600-acre South Siegel roadless area quickly descend 3,500 feet to the Clark Fork. Elk, deer and bald eagles are often seen in the extensive winter habitat, which is also a reintroduction site for bighorn sheep. Highlights during the summer include nesting osprey and a national recreation and nature trail to scenic Cascade Falls.

Summary of Upper Clark Fork Wildlands:
 779,803 acres
Total Amount of Designated Wilderness:
 60,979 acres (7.8%)

JEFF FOOTT

On the National Bison Range.

NORTHERN BITTERROOT DIVIDE

FACING PAGE: GEORGE WUERTHNER; BELOW: JOHN REDDY; RIGHT: GEORGE WUERTHNER

The Bitterroot Mountains stab the sky for 470 miles in a giant arc from Lookout Pass in the northwest to Raynolds Pass near Yellowstone, making them the longest of Montana's mountain ranges. The range's crest marks the most rugged and remote boundary between any two states in the union. The Northern Bitterroot Divide Region, from Lookout Pass to Lost Trail Pass, lies entirely on the Pacific side of the Continental Divide and is actually two distinct subregions. The more subdued northern stretch between Lookout and Lolo passes is broken up with roaded developed lands separated by relatively smaller wildlands. In contrast, the convoluted pinnacles of the southern subregion from Lolo Pass to Lost Trail Pass remain almost completely wild, with unpaved roads touching the crest in only three places.

Above: Below St. Mary's Peak in the Bitterroot Mountains.
Left: Shooting star.

Facing page: Lower Siamese Lake in the Great Burn along the Northern Bitterroot Divide.

49

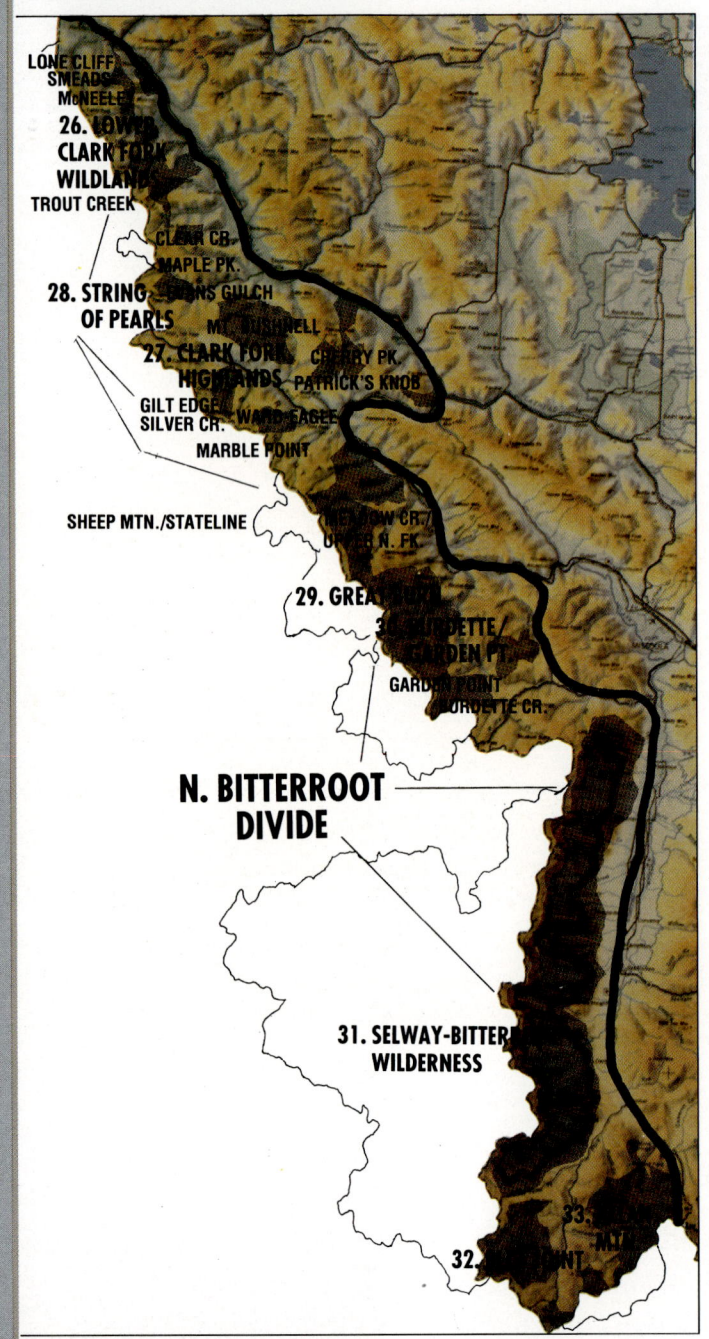

NORTHERN BITTERROOT DIVIDE

Physiographic region COMPLEX Area Name	Area No.†	Montana Gross Acreage	Agency/ Ownership	Management Status
IV. Northern Bitterroot Divide				
LOWER CLARK FORK	26			
Lone Cliff Smeads		6,600	FS	R-NW
McNeeley		7,700	FS	R-NW
CLARK FORK HIGHLANDS	27			
Clear Creek		5,470	FS	R-NW
Mt. Bushnell		43,070	FS	R-NW
Cherry Peak		39,800	FS	R-NW
Patrick's Knob		18,800	FS	R-NW
Marble Point		13,210	FS	R-NW
STRING OF PEARLS	28			
Trout Creek*		31,400	FS	R-NW
Maple Peak*		7,860	FS	R-NW
Evans Gulch		8,830	FS	R-NW
Gilt Edge/Silver Creek		11,200	FS	R-NW
Ward-Eagle		8,570	FS	R-NW
Sheep Mtn./Stateline*		28,000	FS	R-NW
Meadow Cr./Upper N. Fork*		7,200	FS	R-NW
GREAT BURN*	29	98,680	FS	R-NW
BURDETTE/GARDEN POINT	30			
Burdette Creek		16,380	FS	R-NW
Garden Point		6,900	FS	R-NW
SELWAY-BITTERROOT WILDERNESS	31			
Selway-Bitterroot Wilderness*		251,343	FS	W
Contiguous lands		132,078	FS	R-NW
(Contiguous Selway-Bitterroot Wildlands: 383,421 acres)				
BLUE JOINT*	32	65,370	FS	WSA
ALLAN MTN.*	33	102,386	FS	R-NW

Total Wildlands: 910,847 acres. Wilderness: 251,343 acres (27.7%)

---

†For identification purposes in this book only
*Areas with contiguous wildlands in Idaho
**Areas with contiguous wildlands in Wyoming

KEY
Agency Symbols
BLM—Bureau of Land Management
FS—Forest Service
FWS—Fish & Wildlife Service
MDFWP—Montana Dept. of Fish, Wildlife & Parks
NPS—National Park Service
P—Private
S—State
SEA—USDA Science & Education Administration
T—Tribal
TNC—The Nature Conservancy

Management Status Symbols
ACEC—BLM Area of Critical Environmental Concern
BLM WSA—Bureau of Land Management Wilderness Study Area
FPA—Forest Service Further Planning Area
ISA—Instant BLM Study Area
NP—National Park
NRA—National Recreation Area
NWR—National Wildlife Refuge
ONA—BLM Outstanding Natural Area
PP—Private Preserve
R-NW—Roadless-Nonwilderness
RWMA—Recreation & Wildlife Management Area
SP—State Park
TPA—Tribal Primitive Area
TR—Tribal Reserve
TW—Tribal Wilderness
W—Wilderness
WMA—State Wildlife Management Area
WSA—Congressional Wilderness Study Area (Forest Service)

26 Lower Clark Fork Wildlands

Two small roadless areas are situated near Noxon Reservoir on the lower Clark Fork River, downslope from the Bitterroot Divide. The 6,600-acre U-shaped Lone Cliff Smeads area is distinguished by narrow ridges and creek bottoms with enough elk to make it a popular local hunting spot. Chimney Rock and 5,470' Loveland Peak overlook the south bank of the Clark Fork.

During the 1930s, fires swept over what is today the 7,700-acre McNeeley roadless area a few miles south of Lone Cliff Smeads. Most of these mountainsides have not returned to trees. Instead, brushfields and scattered saplings cover the steep slopes, yielding valuable winter forage for deer and elk.

27 Clark Fork Highlands

Due west of Thompson Falls, a series of rocky, subalpine ridges defines the 5,470-acre Clear Creek roadless area. Steep gullies flow into Clear Creek at right angles. Forests of lodgepole pine, Douglas fir and spruce are scheduled for harvest in the upper reaches of the drainage.

The east-west-trending Cabinet-Coeur d'Alene Divide winds through the center of the 43,070-acre Mount Bushnell roadless area, crossing a 5,980' summit with the same name. Densely forested with lodgepole pine from the 1910 burn, Mt. Bushnell also displays an inviting mix of high mountain parks, talus sideslopes and south-facing brushfields. Boggy springs in creek bottoms are favored by summering elk, and deer herds attract stalking mountain lions. Thirty miles of well distributed trails resemble the branching pattern of area streams.

The Cabinet-Coeur d'Alene Divide continues east through the 39,800-acre Cherry Peak roadless area, where it intersects the north-south Eddy Mountain-Greenwood Hill ridgeline. The crossing of two major drainage divides results in an unusual arrangement of topography in the core of these highlands. Glaciation is evident near Eddy Mountain where several tiny alpine lakes are hidden in cirque basins. Vertical relief exceeds 4,500 feet in less than two miles between the Clark Fork and the top of these northern ridges. Patches of subalpine fir and devil's club flourish on wet sites more characteristic of northern Idaho.

Continuing south, the Cabinet-Coeur d'Alene Divide forms the northern boundary of the 18,800-acre Patrick's Knob roadless area. At a fire lookout, it cuts south through the center of this arc-shaped wildland to the Clark Fork River. A thick forest of Douglas fir and larch occupies the west half with more scattered trees to the east. The divide sends streams plummeting 4,000 vertical feet to the river. The entire length of Patrick's Knob is traversed by an east-west fault that offsets rock formations and displaces lesser faults. Wintering bighorn sheep are often seen from the river on steep scree, with elk and deer feeding on more moderate slopes. Of historic interest, an old bootlegger's cabin is tucked away on Fourteen Mile Creek.

A northeast-southwest trending ridge forms the backbone of the 13,210-acre Marble Point roadless area between Superior and St. Regis. Steep ridges with frequent rock outcrops drop 3,800 feet to Dry Creek and to the south side of the Clark Fork. Open faces looking south above Dry Creek are favored elk and deer winter range, comprising fully one third of this wildland.

28 String of Pearls

With the Northern Bitterroot Divide as a common western boundary, a chain of seven roadless pearls unfolds from Trout Creek to Hoodoo Pass.

We begin the chain with a look at the 39,760-acre Trout Creek roadless area, 31,400 acres of which are in Montana. Here the Bitterroot Divide winds road-free for about 15 miles, rising to 6,548' at Black Peak overlooking the head of the East Fork of Trout Creek. The lower reaches of Trout Creek are a veritable elk factory in late spring, with cows dropping and caring for their newborn alongside lush forest openings. Rugged peaks and ridges, tiny tarn lakes below the divide, brushfields left by the 1910 fire and pockets of old growth characterize much of the country. Visitors are attracted by the Settler's Grove of Ancient Cedars Botanical Area, cutthroat and bull trout in the forks of Trout Creek, and the 22-mile Trout Creek loop national recreation trail. But most are drawn by the elusive wapiti during fall hunting season.

The 7,860-acre Montana portion of the Maple Peak interstate "pearl" consists of an east-west ridge at the head of several small drainages entirely within the roadless area. Brushy slopes resulting from the 1910 fire are moderate except near the divide, below which are nestled two tiny

The Montana-Idaho border at the headwaters of Trout Creek.

lakes. Bobcat and lynx live in the forests of pole-sized trees. Rock cairns and chiseled rock mile markers along the divide are left from a 1904 boundary survey.

Alpine glaciation has molded the stateline divide along the west end of the 8,830-acre Evans Gulch roadless area, leaving five ice-scoured lakes. Blosson Lake, popular for fishing, was once connected to Prospect Creek by an irrigation ditch built by early Chinese workers. Most of the land is a series of northeast-southwest ridges and valleys with varied forests growing in life zones spanning 3,500 feet of vertical relief.

With roads from Idaho paralleling the divide, the east face overlooks 11,200 roadless acres in Gilt Edge-Silver Creek. Talus slopes, beargrass meadows and glacial cirques with shallow, fishless potholes lead off from the divide to ridges and valleys covered with mixed coniferous forest. Cougars in the crags and moose in the meadows are among the wild denizens inhabiting these dense forests between the Bitterroot Divide and the St. Regis River.

The compact 8,570-acre Ward Eagle roadless area encompasses a main ridge with glaciated Ward, Eagle and Gold peaks. Bowl-like basins, serrated finger ridges and 14 mountain lakes surrounded by whitebark pine, subalpine fir and scree combine to form breathtaking vistas. In fact, scree and talus slopes make up more than a third of these St. Regis River headwaters. All that survives of a colorful, early gold mining era are an old cabin and dam on Hub Lake.

Prehistoric Indians used the Bitterroot Divide within the Sheep Mountain roadless area for hunting as long ago as 6,000 years. Grinding tools found along the crest point to the existence of extensive whitebark pine forests before the 1910 fire. Snow cornices up to six feet deep drape the divide through early summer, giving rise to major streams flowing east through the 28,000-acre Montana side of this 50,000-acre interstate wildland.

With around 70" of annual precipitation, the high crest is a true subalpine habitat of mountain hemlock and subalpine fir. The State Line Trail contours through open stands of stunted whitebark pine, vestiges of past fires. The influence of these burns is especially striking at the head of Dry Creek, with its graveyards of scattered white snags sticking up through fields of menziesia, ninebark and beargrass. An increasing number of moose along with mountain lion, lynx and wolverine roam these forested mountains, as do summering elk in secluded hanging valleys.

Sheep Mountain is readily accessible from forest roads, yet internally remote. I thought about this atop 7,543' Eagle Cliff Mountain when suddenly a screeching golden eagle soared from the cliff directly below, suspended itself over one of the nine cirque lakes along the foot of the divide, and then vanished just as suddenly. Then came silence—a deep, penetrating feeling of isolation amidst mountains fading from view in every direction.

Only 7,200 acres of the 58,740-acre Meadow Creek-Upper North Fork roadless area lap over the Bitterroot Divide into Montana. Here the divide continues southward with rugged cliff faces rising above lake-filled cirque basins, U-shaped glaciated valleys and an even-aged forest of lodgepole pine downslope, a legacy of the 1910 burn. The State Line national recreation trail passes over centrally-located Illinois Peak, where a metal lookout tower stands guard.

29 The Great Burn

In 1910, raging flames stormed over the Bitterroot Divide only 30 miles west of Missoula, consuming the forest and illuminating the darkness like northern lights from hell. Today, charred snags, barren slopes and expanses of open subalpine tundra lend a distinctive personality to a quarter million acres of interstate wildlands, some 98,680 acres of which drain into Montana's Fish Creek. This primeval land, known as the Great Burn, runs along both sides of the Bitterroot Divide for 40 miles. Induced by the 1910 fire, the subalpine tundra of the Great Burn lies at a much lower elevation than one would expect at this latitude. In striking contrast, centuries-old western redcedar grow in cathedral-like settings along shaded pools meandering through verdant, mossy beds of sword and maidenhair ferns.

I sat alone on top of a remote, windblown summit deep within the Great Burn, and I wondered what it is that really set the land before me apart from other wild places. Below me stretched a "graveyard" of ghost-white snags, remnants of the great inferno. Images came to mind of cas-

BILL CUNNINGHAM

Above: *The 1910 Burn has induced a low-elevation tundra along the Bitterroot Divide.*

Facing page: *In the Great Burn area of Lolo/Clearwater National Forest.*

cading waterfalls, clear mountain lakes hidden in deep cirques, blazing yellow larch in the fall, crimson heather adorning the slopes of glacial headwalls, the vast subalpine tundra of high, open ridges, of elk rearing their young in lush hanging valleys, of goats hopping nimbly along sheer rock cliffs.

It was then that I knew. The Great Burn, unlike the majority of our remaining wildlands where one looks down on towns, farms and roads, inspires a feeling of complete wildness. I've had the same feeling in the middle of the Bob Marshall.

30 Burdette/Garden Point

Examination of scars in ancient trees within the 16,380-acre Burdette Creek wild area in the Fish Creek drainage reveals a past natural fire frequency of 37 years. Because of fire suppression, it has been twice that long since the last major fire. Differing from those in most mountainous wildlands, past fires here have transformed almost all of Burdette Creek into superb wildlife winter range where some 400 elk feed on the succulent new growth of serviceberry, ceanothus and upland willow. In an enlightened reversal of past policy, the Forest Service is deliberately burning nearly 500 Burdette Creek acres per year for the next decade. The idea is to establish a mosaic of verdant shrubs for forage along with dense tree canopy for hiding cover.

A four-mile trail cushioned with larch needles stays close to bubbling Burdette Creek, bending around gigantic old-growth larches. Every so often the forest opens to a grand view of the drainage with its sharp ridges and expansive brushfields interspersed with dense stringers of Douglas fir in the protected draws and north-facing slopes. Steep grassy ridges between Burdette and Lupine creeks support classic ponderosa pine parks with some of the fire-resistant veterans towering more than 100 feet.

The Fish Creek-Petty Creek Divide separates the adjacent 6,900-acre Garden Point roadless area from the northeast corner of Burdette Creek. Only the upper reaches of moderately steep, heavily forested east-west ridges and east-flowing streams remain unroaded.

31 Selway-Bitterroot Wilderness

The 251,343-acre Bitterroot portion of the Selway-Bitterroot is Montana's contribution to this vast Wilderness of 1,337,681 acres. An additional 132,078 acres of unroaded canyons along the east face of the Bitterroots bring this total contiguous wildland in Montana to 383,421 acres.

GEORGE WUERTHNER

53

ABOVE: JOHN REDDY; INSET: JEFF FOOTT

Above: Ponderosa pine frames the rugged upper reaches of Bass Creek in the Selway-Bitterroot Wilderness.
Inset: Bighorn sheep.
Facing page: Trapper Peak.

Hundreds of peaks separate more than 30 remote drainages for nearly 90 miles along a dramatic mountain front stretching from the South Fork of Lolo Creek south to where ridges break abruptly into the West Fork of the Bitterroot River. From the lofty vantage point of any of the high 9,000' to 10,000' peaks the first impression is of barren rock—granite, gneiss and schist—from the jumbled crest of the range to the valley floor. Then the eye begins to focus on detail. Ridges on the horizon start to reveal sheer walls, cliffs, tumbling waterfalls, hanging valleys, subalpine lake basins and a glaciated terrain so rugged that, in comparison, most other Montana mountain ranges seem like gently rolling hills.

The major glaciers probably receded less than 10,000 years ago, leaving deep, steep-walled east-west canyons, each with a classic U-shape from Pleistocene valley glaciation. With more than a mile of vertical relief in a short distance, the variety of vegetation is equally impressive. From creeks to crest there is old-growth western redcedar and tenacious, slow-growing alpine larch. Of special interest is an unusual association of western larch and alpine larch at the same elevation on the extreme northern tip near Lolo Peak. This is one of the few places known where hybridization between the two species has occurred.

Although much of this rough landscape is treeless and austere, there are surprising pockets of wildlife. Elk summer in lush basins along the divide and hide in heavily forested canyons during hunting season. The native bighorn sheep population in Sheephead and Watchtower creeks at the southern end of the roadless expanse is genetically pure, a rarity in the United States. The herd has a unique learned migration pattern between winter and summer range that would likely be lost if interrupted.

The east-facing Montana side of the Wilderness is so rugged that almost all of its visitors are restricted to the shorelines of lakes and to the bottoms of canyons. Each of the dozens of glaciated Bitterroot canyons holds its own special discoveries—from the natural arch in Blodgett to a massive landslide across Nelson Creek that backed up Nelson Lake.

32 *Blue Joint*

The Nez Perce road is all that separates the triangular 65,370-acre Blue Joint wild country from the Selway-Bitterroot Wilderness. Even so, Blue Joint is part of another vast wildland—the 2,230,000-acre Frank Church-River of No Return Wilderness that extends deep into central Idaho with 17 miles of common boundary along the Bitterroot Divide. History comes alive with a segment of the Southern Nez Perce Indian Trail traversing this portion of the divide.

With elevations ranging from 4,900' to 8,600', half of the Blue Joint exceeds 7,000'. The rocky, grassy spine of Razorback Ridge splits the country into northwest and southeast portions. Douglas fir and ponderosa pine grow at warmer, lower elevations with lodgepole pine on cooler midslopes on up to whitebark pine clinging to high, narrow ridges. Forest fires in the late 1800s burned most of the Blue Joint drainage, producing a vast even-aged forest of spindly lodgepole pine—in contrast with the surrounding forest. Large, open meadows, a rarity in the Bitterroot Mountains, occupy the headwaters of Deer and Blue Joint creeks. Notable features include 7,922' Castle Rock, remnant of a volcanic plug, and a natural rock arch east of the confluence of Jack the Ripper and Blue Joint creeks.

The indigenous, genetically pure bighorn sheep herd in the southern breaks of the Selway-Bitterroot Wilderness also uses the northern edge of Blue Joint near Castle Rock, where the defense of rocky terrain is used for lambing. In recognition of these wild resources, Congress classified Blue Joint as a Wilderness Study Area in Senator Metcalf's 1977 Montana Wilderness Study Act.

33 *Allan Mountain*

As the Bitterroot Divide swings northeast toward Lost Trail Pass it becomes the backbone of another large interstate roadless area known as Allan Mountain, 102,386 acres of which drain into the upper West Fork of the Bitterroot River. The centerpiece of this wildland is spectacular Overwhich Falls, close to where the stream cuts back through erosive soils and bedrock to capture the headwaters of Fault Creek.

About 60 percent of the Allan Mountain country lies above 7,000', where the forest is mostly lodgepole pine, subalpine fir and whitebark pine. Here the alpine larch reaches the southern limit of its range, grasping steep narrow ridges. Big grassy parks favored by deer and elk were created by fires in 1917 and again in 1919. Native cutthroat abound in the cold, clear waters of rapid streams.

Summary of North Bitterroot Divide Wildlands:
 910,847 acres
Total Amount of Designated Wilderness:
 251,343 acres (27.7%)

WAYNE MUMFORD

UPPER MISSOURI/GREAT DIVIDE

LEFT: RONALD J. GLOVAN;
BELOW: DIANE ENSIGN;
RIGHT: GILDEMEISTER

The Upper Missouri/Great Divide region includes the intermountain basins and isolated yet intimate ranges of southwest Montana. It is bounded on the west by the southern half of Montana's Continental Divide, from near Helena south to Monida Pass. From rolling grasslands to some of Montana's loftiest peaks, these little-known wild headwaters give birth to some of the Big Sky's best known blue ribbon streams: the Big Hole and Beaverhead rivers.

Above: The stable flows of the Big Hole River rely upon its wild and undisturbed headwaters.
Left: Wild geranium.

Facing page: Barb Lake, East Pioneers.

57

UPPER MISSOURI/GREAT DIVIDE

Physiographic region COMPLEX Area Name	Area No.†	Montana Gross Acreage	Agency/ Ownership	Management Status
V. Upper Missouri/Great Divide				
HELENA WILDLANDS	34			
Black Mtn.		13,300	FS	R-NW
Jericho Mtn.		9,439	FS	R-NW
BOULDER BATHOLITH WILDLANDS	35			
Whitetail/Haystack		77,160	FS	R-NW
O'Neil Creek		6,511	FS	R-NW
HUMBUG SPIRES	36	11,335	BLM	ISA
HIGHLANDS	37			
Highlands		20,921	FS	R-NW
Basin Creek		9,888	FS	R-NW
TOBACCO ROOTS	38			
Tobacco Root Mtns.		98,322	FS/BLM	R-NW
Potosi		5,465	FS	R-NW
RUBY MTNS.	39	28,247	BLM	BLM WSA
BLACKTAIL MTNS.	40	17,479	BLM	BLM WSA
HENNEBERRY RIDGE	41	9,807	BLM	BLM WSA
MCCARTNEY MTN./SANDY HOLLOW	42	17,580	BLM	R-NW
FLEECER MTNS.	43	52,287	FS	R-NW
EAST PIONEER MTNS.	44			
East Pioneers		147,428	FS/BLM	R-NW, BLM WSA
Call Mtn.		10,184	FS	R-NW
Cattle Gulch Ridge		19,776	FS	R-NW
WEST PIONEERS	45	239,572	FS	WSA, R-NW
ANACONDA-PINTLER COMPLEX	46			
Anaconda-Pintler Wilderness		157,874	FS	W
Swift & Needle Creek		1,829	FS	R-NW
Sapphires		117,030	FS	WSA, R-NW
North Carp		12,042	FS	R-NW
Upper East Fork		7,361	FS	R-NW
Storm Lake		14,720	FS	R-NW
North Big Hole		56,889	FS	R-NW
(Contiguous Anaconda-Pintler/Sapphires Wildlands: 367,745 acres)				
Beaver Lake		13,474	FS	R-NW
ANDERSON MTN.*	47	31,401	FS	R-NW
WEST BIG HOLE	48			
West Big Hole*		33,977	FS	R-NW
Saginaw Creek		8,493	FS	R-NW
SOUTH BIG HOLE	49	57,944	FS	R-NW
LEMHI-BANNOCK/GREAT DIVIDE WILDLANDS	50			
Bear Creek		8,252	FS	R-NW
Goat Mtn.*		9,454	FS	R-NW
TENDOY MTNS. COMPLEX	51			
Tendoys		68,801	FS, BLM	R-NW
Sourdough Peak		14,843	FS	R-NW
ITALIAN PEAKS*	52	91,277	FS	R-NW
LIMA PEAKS	53			
Garfield Mtn.*		42,701	FS	R-NW
Four Eyes Canyon		8,237	FS	R-NW

Total Wildlands: 1,651,300 acres. Wilderness: 157,874 acres (9.6%)

†For identification purposes in this book only
*Areas with contiguous wildlands in Idaho
**Areas with contiguous wildlands in Wyoming

KEY

Agency Symbols
BLM—Bureau of Land Management
FS—Forest Service
FWS—Fish & Wildlife Service
MDFWP—Montana Dept. of Fish, Wildlife & Parks
NPS—National Park Service
P—Private
S—State
SEA—USDA Science & Education Administration
T—Tribal
TNC—The Nature Conservancy

Management Status Symbols
ACEC—BLM Area of Critical Environmental Concern
BLM WSA—Bureau of Land Management Wilderness Study Area
FPA—Forest Service Further Planning Area
ISA—Instant BLM Study Area
NP—National Park
NRA—National Recreation Area
NWR—National Wildlife Refuge
ONA—BLM Outstanding Natural Area
PP—Private Preserve
R-NW—Roadless-Nonwilderness
RWMA—Recreation & Wildlife Management Area
SP—State Park
TPA—Tribal Primitive Area
TR—Tribal Reserve
TW—Tribal Wilderness
W—Wilderness
WMA—State Wildlife Management Area
WSA—Congressional Wilderness Study Area (Forest Service)

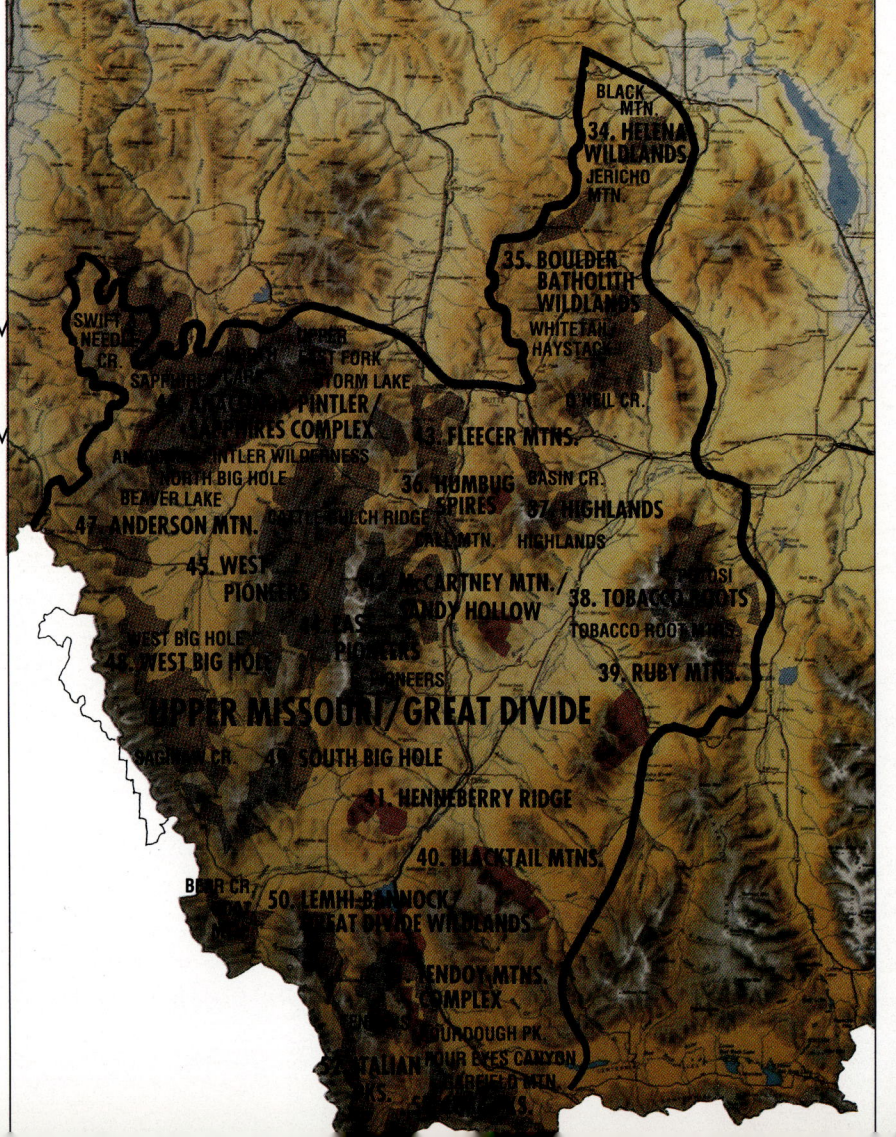

34 Helena Wildlands

It is possible, indeed enjoyable, to walk southwest from the city limits of Montana's capital city along the Helena Skyline national recreation trail to the 13,300-acre Black Mountain roadless area. The amount of wildlife and natural diversity within this compact wildland is astonishing. Dense forests, wet springs and grassy parks combine as year-round habitat for up to 400 elk as well as moose, mule deer, lion, bobcat, marten, fox and black bear.

At 7,223', the open top of Colorado Mountain connects to a saddle ridge through mature lodgepole pine to Black Mountain, which is crowned with a rock pile graced by a delicate little aspen. Just below the summit another rock outcrop provides a more open view, especially to the southeast toward expansive Blackhall Meadows and the head of Colorado Gulch. This point also features a perfect sitting rock with a comfortable stone backrest!

The 9,439-acre Jericho Mountain roadless area is split by the Continental Divide and bounded by Tenmile Creek to the immediate west of Black Mountain. Here the Continental Divide National Scenic Trail traverses rolling lodgepole pine/subalpine fir forests for about seven miles at elevations averaging 7,300'. Wildlife use is year-long but the streams are only seasonal.

35 Boulder Batholith Wildlands

The 77,160-acre Whitetail/Haystack roadless area northeast of Butte is a case study in wilderness restoration. First came the removal of a powerline, which unified two previously separate wildlands. Then came the closing of a controversial logging road as a result of appeals from local citizens.

The generally subdued landscape is dominated by 8,862' Haystack Mountain and 8,475' Whitetail Peak, from which numerous broad ridges radiate. The huge natural basin of Whitetail Park holds a marsh so diverse that its flora changes distinctly every 20 feet, with an elevation difference of only six inches.

Piles of Boulder Batholith granite form small mounds topped with spires, pinnacles and rounded rock ridges. A fascinating geologic feature of these flat benchlands is the "Moving Boulders." Frost action pushes them along, leaving behind a "walking" path. Rusted haying equipment is all that remains of early 1900s homesteads in mountain parks today enjoyed by summering elk, moose and mule deer.

Straddling the Continental Divide only two miles east of Butte, the 6,511-acre O'Neil Creek roadless area drains into Delmoe Lake—which separates it from Whitetail/Haystack. The steep, rugged west slope drops 2,000 feet from the divide to the valley floor. Rolling forests of lodgepole pine and Douglas fir on the east side are dotted with granite outcrops of Boulder Batholith topped with spires of rounded rocks. Lush stream bottoms with willow, sedges, water lilies and cattails are favored by beaver and moose.

36 Humbug Spires

The Humbug Spires Wilderness Study Area managed by the Bureau of Land Management is 11,335 acres of dense forests, meadows and canyons on the edge of the Big Hole River Valley between the Highland and East Pioneer ranges. The main artery—Moose Creek—flows through a narrow boulder-strewn canyon, changing to a series of pools, beaver ponds and cascades. The steepest waterfalls form a barrier between trout in the lower stream and native cutthroat in its upper reaches. Rare plants on the brink of extinction are Idaho sedge, Kelsey's milk-vetch and Rocky Mountain Douglasia.

Weathering and erosion of the central granitic core have produced the unique spires for which Humbug is named. The size and distribution of these granite spires is unequalled in the Northwest, providing what is likely the highest-quality hard-rock climbing in Montana. At least nine spires rise between 300 and 600 feet, with more than 50 less than 300 feet high. The largest individual spire is called "The Wedge." Another spire, "The Crown," is overhung on all sides and has never been climbed. Its top is surely among the only truly untracked wilderness in Montana.

GEORGE WUERTHNER

Humbug Spires Primitive Area.

JOHN REDDY

The Highland Mountains.

37 The Highlands

The towering mountains of the compact 20,921-acre Highlands roadless area serve as a spectacular backdrop to Butte. Red and Table mountains exceed 10,000', with the scalloped summits of the Continental Divide twisting through the range. Gentle grass-covered foothills and rounded ridges climb abruptly to the high peaks dispatching steep drainages northward. Lower north-facing slopes are covered with lodgepole pine, whereas cirque basins are dotted with marshes, talus and varied alpine flora. The deep green of Emerald Lake accents the red rock of nearby Red Mountain. Nutritious alpine forage, ideal for bighorn sheep, gives native Highlands rams the fastest horn growth of any herd in Montana.

The Great Divide winds through the 9,888-acre Basin Creek roadless area on the north side of the Highlands. The absence of roads helps protect Butte's Basin Creek municipal watershed, which occupies most of this subdued, rock-strewn lodgepole/Douglas fir forest. Huge gray-white granite boulders define ridges that plunge into countless V-shaped valleys thick with aspen, alder and willow.

38 The Tobacco Roots

The higher reaches of the isolated Tobacco Root Range south of Whitehall is segmented by the Forest Service into eight subunits. With some small adjacent Bureau of Land Management parcels, the total reaches 98,322 roadless acres. This fragmentation is the product of old mines and mining roads. Still, wildness prevails in what is perhaps the densest complex of high peaks in Montana, where 26 rocky pinnacles rise above 10,000'. The most rugged topography in the range lies along the glacial cirque head of Indian Creek, which supplies much of Sheridan's municipal water.

From mixed grassland, sagebrush and juniper winter range for elk, antelope and deer, the country ascends to lodgepole, Douglas fir and spruce on up to whitebark pine and finally to matted tundra in the alpine. Small wet meadows, often bounded by large outcrops of granite, are found in every U-shaped valley.

After climbing 10,353' Middle Mountain, I wrote, "This central summit allows a magnificent view—literally 360 degrees of lofty peaks, hanging valleys and alpine lakes to feast one's eyes upon. Unable to see Louise Lake from the top I dropped to a saddle about 1/4 mile northeast and there were the goats—50 yards downslope and 10 in number, including three tiny snow-white kids, flowing in unison like a soft white ribbon."

In contrast to the sharp peaks of the main Tobacco Roots, the eastern slopes of the range within the 5,465-acre Potosi roadless area are relatively gentle. Lodgepole pine and grassy parks cover these undulating ridges and dissected foothills where raptors and mountain lions hunt their prey.

39 Ruby Mountains

Only 15 miles east of Dillon, the Ruby Mountains Wilderness Study Area encompasses 28,247 acres of steep, dissected terrain managed by the Bureau of Land Management. A main north-south ridge forms the backbone of the range, with the north end a jumbled maze of 20 drainages. Springs are scarce in these dry mountains, so snowmelt is all that flows through the canyons. The southern portion is cut by many draws, but is less steep, with aspen groves and streamside meadows.

About 80 percent of the Rubys is forested with Douglas fir, lodgepole and spruce. More than half of the land is above 8,000', causing trees to be stunted in a harsh environment of shallow soils. The upper slopes display vast, pure stands of limber pine interspersed with small parks—a vegetative type more common far to the south.

Complex geology includes free-standing rock walls, caves, cliffs, talus and a major ridgeline apexing at 9,391' Ruby Peak. Although a few elk dwell here year-around, these mountains are best known as superior mule deer and blue grouse country.

60

40 Blacktail Mountains

The 17,479-acre Blacktail Mountains Wilderness Study Area managed by the Bureau of Land Management is the wild core of a dramatic upthrust 12 miles south of Dillon. The range is dominated by a high northwest-southeast trending plateau extending for 12 miles. Streams flow northeast through deep, timbered canyons with sheer cliffs and headwalls. Scattered forests in protected, north-facing pockets are a mosaic of Douglas fir, limber pine and spruce. Sagebrush grows above and below timberline. Matted tundra-like plants and grasses lend an alpine flavor to the wide and windy central plateau that rises to the barely discernable high point of 9,477'. Jake Canyon shelters winter range for about 130 elk with perhaps twice that number relying on secluded basins the rest of the year.

Special discoveries await the visitor, from the surprisingly lush, green bottom of the South Fork of Riley Creek to the striking red rock at the head of the South Fork of Ashbough Canyon. An amateur geologist would have a field day studying complex folded and faulted structures.

41 Henneberry Ridge

The Bureau of Land Management's (BLM) Henneberry Ridge Wilderness Study Area is 9,807 acres of mostly open, well dissected prairie just south of historic Bannack. The prominent eight-mile-long ridge after which the roadless area is named is distinguished by eroded remnants of sedimentary rock. Steep slopes lead to a central bench with a maze of hills, ridges and coulees trending northwest toward Grasshopper Creek. Mule deer and antelope use this broken sagebrush steppe year-around, with elk wintering in Madigan Gulch.

42 McCartney Mountain/Sandy Hollow

The Big Hole River bends around a 17,580-acre chunk of undeveloped BLM land delineated by 8,364' McCartney Mountain on the north and Sandy Hollow to the southeast. Lower Sandy Hollow contains drive alignment cairns and rock walls used for an early pishkun or buffalo jump near the Big Hole. Although livestock grazing and past mining use are evident in places, the overall landscape remains wild, especially in the steep, thickly-forested ridges and deep canyons leading south from Bell Peak and McCartney Mountain. Elk calve in this more remote northern section.

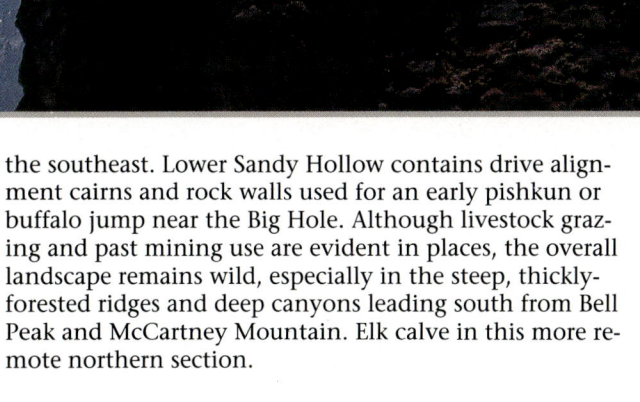

JOHN REDDY

The Tobacco Root Mountains

61

GEORGE WUERTHNER

43 Fleecer Mountains

The open, rounded 9,436' top of Mt. Fleecer marks the high point of a 37,287-acre roadless area southwest of Butte. North along the Continental Divide, 8,383' Burnt Mountain rises as the most prominent landmark. Turn-of-the-century charcoal woodcutting is evident nearby. As part of the most intensively hunted district in Montana, Fleecer conjures images of an orange-clad army in search of elk. Jerry Creek provides primary access, with its upper reaches an undulating basin. Smaller creeks with beaver dams meander through wet-willow meadows. This long, narrow series of ridges and side drainages is covered mostly with lodgepole pine along with spacious grassy parks on Hogback and Fleecer.

Long, wide slopes flank the rounded rocky ridges of Granulated and Little Granulated mountains and of 9,116' Dickie Peak in the 15,000-acre Granulated Mountain roadless area. This partially glaciated land of lodgepole and big parks drains into the Big Hole River while providing a spring and summer home for part of the Fleecer elk herd. A five-acre pocket of rare subalpine larch adorns the north slope of Granulated Mountain.

44 East Pioneer Mountains

The strongly glaciated 147,428-acre East Pioneers roadless area is a geological puzzle with sharp peaks and steep walls. Rocky cirque basins hold more than 30 sparkling trout-filled lakes bounded by jagged summits and U-shaped glacial trough valleys. Wet seeps and meadows reveal higher water tables in the southern portion of the range.

A mile of vertical relief rises abruptly from Rock Creek to the imposing main dividing ridge, slicing longitudinally for 25 serpentine miles. The crest is marked by the highest peaks on the Beaverhead Forest—11,154' Tweedy and Torrey at 11,147'. On the west side, steep, dissected sidehills break rapidly to the Wise River. East slopes drop more gradually along rolling foothills to the Big Hole.

Large differences in elevation contribute to a wide variety of plants and animals. On a typical hike to the high country you would likely begin your journey in a grass-and-sagebrush park. Walking up through a lodgepole/subalpine forest, you would eventually top a windswept ridge or headwall with pure whitebark pine. Upper timberline would be around 9,000' with hearty shrub-like trees and alpine tundra. Here the only sounds would be wind, a pika's whistle or the cry of a raptor.

Mountain goats make a good living along cliff faces from Torrey Mountain northeast to a linear plateau north of Canyon Creek, known as "Elephant's Trunk" because of its shape. Sawtooth and Hidden lakes harbor colorful golden trout, and the rare arctic grayling fins the icy waters of Grayling Lake.

Isolated by intervening roads, the 10,184-acre Call Mountain area is a rocky, roadless block of country on the east end of the Pioneers. Steep slopes mantled with lodgepole surround 9,010' Call Mountain and two subalpine lakes, one home to cutthroat and the other to grayling.

On the northeast corner of the range is the topographically varied 19,776-acre Cattle Gulch roadless area, where narrow, rocky ridges separate gentle valleys. To the north, steep canyons plunge to the Big Hole River. Limestone cliffs, caves and spires add variety to a landscape equally divided between lodgepole and sagebrush/grassland. Open south-facing aspects with mountain mahogany on lower slopes attract wintering elk and mule deer. Bighorn sheep inhabit lower Cattle Gulch throughout the year.

45 West Pioneers

The more rounded West Pioneers, on the sunrise side of the expansive Big Hole Valley, is so strikingly different from the ruggedly alpine East Pioneers that it's hard to believe that the same major mountain mass encompasses both areas. The two ranges are divided by Wise River, a major north-flowing tributary of the Big Hole. The 148,000-acre West Pioneers Montana Wilderness Study Area is the wild core of a 239,572-acre roadless resource—one of Montana's largest contiguous wildlands without any formal Wilderness protection.

The northern crest overlooks several sparkling lakes, most of them excellent fisheries due to their remoteness. With steep, Rocky Mountain goat rocks in the north and gentler terrain in the south, the country attains 9,497' atop Stine Mountain. Seventy percent of the high-quality water produced comes from snowmelt rushing through wet meadows and parks to the Big Hole. Sagebrush and grassland complement dense lodgepole forest, with spruce in the bottoms. Giant specimens of whitebark pine along windblown ridges are some of the oldest in Montana. Western larch grows near the head of Osborne Creek—easternmost extension of the species. The longest-living stand of lodgepole pine known—500 years old—survives in the undisturbed Effie Creek drainage. An added ecological value is a pure-strain lake population of arctic grayling, likely the last outside Alaska. They reproduce in Odell, Schwinegar and one Bobcat lake. Old Tim Creek, lined by picturesque meadows, contains remnant pure-strain native cutthroat.

The country is large and diverse enough to provide year-around elk habitat, from foothill winter range to calving grounds, from summer grazing to fall security in lodgepole thickets. The West Pioneers is one of the best and last places in Montana where a hunter can pursue wild elk in wild country with a good chance of bagging a trophy bull. Overall, these gentle mountains have a comfortable, sublime feeling—as inviting to the human visitor as it is for the newborn elk calf.

46 Anaconda-Pintler Wilderness/ Sapphires Complex

With 50 miles of the Great Divide as its roadless spine, the 367,745-acre Anaconda-Pintler Wilderness complex is among the seven largest wildlands in Montana. The 157,874-acre Anaconda-Pintler Wilderness is the central jewel in this wild crown, surrounded by contigu-

BILL CUNNINGHAM

Above: From Congdon Peak, the high crest of the Sapphires winds southwest, joining with the Continental Divide.

Facing page: The West Pioneers and the Big Hole Valley.

ous unroaded lands that include the Sapphire Range—the crest of which is a northern spur off the Continental Divide.

The remote wilderness core is bisected by the Great Divide where it makes an east-west deviation from its predominantly north-south orientation. A vertical mile separates remnants of old-growth forests in the lower valleys from the highest summit in the Anaconda Range—10,793' West Goat Peak—where the classic signatures of past glaciation dominate the landscape. Only the hardiest rock-hugging lichens and mosses can live on the exposed ridges and austere peaks above 10,000'.

These secluded stretches of the Great Divide give birth to some of the world's finest trout streams, including Rock Creek and the Big Hole River. Cirques with dozens of alpine lakes, U-shaped forested valleys and glacial moraines combine to form a wilderness wonderland. Perpetual snowbanks feed tumbling streams that rest only briefly as trout-filled pools in deep canyons. Denizens of this high country include mountain goats, flying squirrels and 13 varieties of raptors.

To the north the contiguous 117,030-acre Sapphire Mountains wildland is well named, for it is indeed a precious gem of wildness. Most of these gentle mountains are within a congressional Montana Wilderness Study Area. Exposed bedrock, rubble and granite spires alternating with open whitebark pine and subalpine larch lend an alpine flavor to 40 miles of high crest that cuts through the center of the unroaded expanse to its intersection with the Continental Divide. Glacial scouring has carved steep, rocky basins that hold 15 small lakes and countless potholes in the headwaters of the west-side Bitterroot River and east-side Rock Creek. The roadlessness of this linear wildland safeguards spacious streamside meadows and old-growth forests uncommon elsewhere in the range. The land is big, diverse and wild enough to support at least 1,000 elk, along with moose, bighorn sheep, wolverine and pileated woodpecker.

An excerpt from the journal of conservationist Bud Moore during an extended backpack along the crest gives insight into the real treasure of the Sapphires: "…the forest is primeval and intimate yet a vista here and there lets the traveler orient to the great space around him. Glimpses of the high country far to the south spur him on and lend bigness to the country."

Roadless lands along the present northern boundary of the Anaconda-Pintler Wilderness begin as gentle forested slopes leading to bedrock cliffs and sheer avalanche chutes filled with scree, ending at tiny lakes surrounded by lush meadows. One Hundred Acre Meadow is high enough to be in the tundra life zone, yet it looks like a lower-elevation park.

Majestic 10,641' Mt. Evans on the Continental Divide towers over the 14,720-acre Storm Lake roadless area on the northeast corner of the Wilderness. Dozens of glistening blue-black tarns are hidden in scoured cirques below which U-shaped glacial valleys end in undulating moraines. Black and gray crags fall sharply off horn peaks along the divide, where both mountain goats and snowfields stay most of the year.

The north end of the Big Hole Valley meets 56,889 roadless acres of rolling, timbered foothills with gently rounded ridges and open parks cut by streams originating in the Anaconda-Pintler Wilderness. An uneven-aged lodgepole pine forest is broken by small, secret openings ideal for elk spring calving and summer range. The country is high, so usually by mid-November most of the elk have migrated across the Great Divide to their winter range in the Bitterroot.

A key feature in the North Big Hole is a large, subalpine meadow known as Clam Valley. Meandering Clam Creek cuts deeply through the center of the open park, providing habitat for a unique species of freshwater clam that may have been isolated by the retreat of the last glacier.

This is the Anaconda-Pintler/Sapphires complex—a vast unbroken wildland that remains wild and free from the Skalkaho to the Big Hole.

The 13,474-acre Beaver Lake roadless area is separated from the Anaconda-Pintler Wilderness by the most heavily-logged land in the upper Big Hole. More than 60 percent of these slightly glaciated, moderately rolling lodgepole forests have been developed since 1979, with additional timber sales planned. The country provides undisturbed migration routes for elk.

47 Anderson Mountain

The Anderson Mountain roadless area brings us back to the Bitterroot Range where its crest, the Montana-Idaho border, and the Continental Divide are one

CHARLES E. KAY

Above: *The high, rolling grasslands of the Great Divide lead toward the Italian Peaks.*

Facing page: *Toward Mt. Warren, Anaconda-Pintler.*

and the same. The 31,401-acre roadless Montana side, east of the Divide, begins as steep subalpine forest dropping to tight V-shaped drainages separated by narrow, slightly rounded ridges. The country is thickly covered with elk-hiding lodgepole. Spruce and small meadows line myriad streams that eventually feed into the Big Hole.

48 West Big Hole

Ranchers and sportsmen have long proposed protection against roads and logging in the higher, middle and lower slopes of this Continental Divide wild country. Rising from the sunset side of the broad Big Hole Valley west of Wisdom and Jackson, the snowy southern Bitterroot Mountains reach over 10,000' along the divide before dropping sharply into Idaho. From sagebrush plains the lodgepole-mantled foothills of Montana's 133,977-acre share of the West Big Hole rise gradually, merging into glaciated U-shaped canyons and finally jutting steeply to the Great Divide. Especially impressive is the rock-strewn mass of centrally-located 10,620' Homer Youngs Peak, which looks down on the Continental Divide from the east.

Nearly 30 deep-blue alpine lakes are cupped in lush hanging valleys where wildflowers achieve their colorful explosion by mid-July along the edge of lingering snowfields. At lower elevations one can savor the quiet joy of a subalpine meadow and experience the peace of a winding stream with deep pools full of brookies that seem made for a kid's first fishing trip. Wildlife are as diverse as the landscape, with black bears, mountain lions, elk, deer, moose, goats and wolverines. This breathtaking 40-mile-long stretch of high country is an exceptional producer of pure water for ranchers, anglers, fish and other downstream users.

Encircled by forest roads, the 8,493-acre Saginaw Creek roadless area on the southeastern slopes of the West Big Hole centers on the Big Hole-Selway Divide. Sagebrush/grassland mixed with moose bogs and rolling lodgepole/Douglas fir forests surround the rocky point of 8,898' Selway Mountain.

49 South Big Hole

Rising from the south end of the valley, the 57,944-acre South Big Hole roadless area is a mellow blend of wet meadows, grassy parks and dense lodgepole hiding cover that seems to have been made for elk. Perhaps the greatest attribute of this country is its remoteness—it's a long way from anywhere.

From a hilltop on the north end, during a recent visit, my companion and I could see hundreds of elk in at least a

JOHN REDDY

BILL CUNNINGHAM

dozen groups grazing undisturbed out in the open. Amidst spitting spring snow, the lifting clouds began to unveil a stunning panorama of unspoiled landscape, bringing with it the overpowering feeling of immense, uncluttered space.

The Big Hole Divide slits the country from northeast to southwest as it passes over several talus-topped summits above 9,000', including 9,812' Bloody Dick Peak. Rock-strewn ridges with gnarled whitebark pine and cliff faces are home to a couple dozen mountain goats. A small cirque and rough, rocky shoreline surround Peterson Lake, lending an alpine character to the basin despite its relatively low elevation. Treeless meadows formed by eons of soil deposition behind beaver dams are cut by deep, meandering creeks teeming with pan-sized brookies. Sandhill cranes stop over in these secluded valleys during summer.

50 Lemhi-Bannock/Great Divide Wildlands

Two small wildlands occupy most of the highlands along the Continental Divide between historic Lemhi and Bannock passes. The 8,252-acre Bear Creek roadless area encompasses the deep, V-shaped upper canyons of its namesake drainage. The divide rises to 9,400', overlooking long rounded ridges that descend to foothills used by elk, mule deer and antelope.

The 9,454-acre Montana portion of the Goat Mountain roadless area is similar to adjacent Bear Creek with its open parks and narrow valley bottoms. Drainages flow east, resulting in pronounced north-south aspect differences on the opposite, moderately steep valley sidewalls. Lithic scatterings of agate tell of early Indian hunting parties along the divide.

51 Tendoy Mountains

The north-south-trending Tendoy Mountains rise sharply to the west of the Red Rock River near Lima. The BLM and Forest Service have segmented 83,644 roadless acres into six units. Actually, the eastern five areas are one contiguous 68,801-acre wildland extending 20 miles along the crest of the range. Only two low-standard roads penetrate the interior from the east.

On the north end, the steep, rugged Bell and Limekiln canyons present a complex study of the effects of erosion with 700-foot-high cliff faces, ledges, talus, caves and rock walls. Because it is a free-standing rock wall, Wedding Ring Rock in Limekiln is of special geological interest. A mosaic of grass, sagebrush and forested ridges provides exceptional year-round mule deer habitat.

JOHN REDDY

Southward, McKenzie Canyon is typical of a maze of steep, rocky canyons that descend to rolling, dissected foothills. Douglas fir and lodgepole grow higher up and on north-facing slopes. The sedimentary walls of Sourdough Cave display Indian pictographs. Gentle alluvial fans and sage-covered hills surround Timber Butte, named for its mantle of Douglas fir. The southeast corner of the Tendoys is dominated by the highest and most prominent landmark in the range—9,674' Dixon Mountain—with its steep, rocky east face overlooking the broad alluvial fans of Red Rock Valley.

Of the more than 40 minor, seasonally dry drainages that flow out of the southern Tendoys, only Hidden Pasture Creek is large enough to carry water year-round. Open sagebrush, grassland and patches of Douglas fir and mountain mahogany are used all year by mule deer and antelope and by elk during the winter and spring. In the southwest corner of the range the 14,843-acre Sourdough Mountain roadless area is cut off from the main Tendoy Mountains wildland by roads to the north and east. Sourdough Peak, at 9,571', rises prominently above wide expanses of dry rolling ridges and foothills, breaking steeply to deep, southwest-flowing canyons.

52 Italian Peaks

The high, wide and dry Italian Peaks wildland is truly Montana's "hidden corner" at the state's southernmost extremity. The centerpiece is Italian Peak itself; a 10,998' massif of the Continental Divide with a sheer, overpowering 2,000' precipice of shattered limestone. Distinctive ridges define the upper Nicholia Basin where scattered clumps of whitebark pine and spruce surround wet tarn meadows with undulating "kame and kettle"-like topography. Most of these southern Bitterroots are either above timberline or interspersed with isolated patches of lodgepole pine and Douglas fir on cooler slopes.

The divide is a narrow, gently sloping grassy ridgetop in the northern reaches, becoming sharper with steep, rocky cirque headwalls south of Morrison Lake. From 11,141' Eighteenmile Peak—the highest point on Montana's Continental Divide—one gets a sense of how vast is this more than 300,000-acre roadless area, 91,277 acres of which drain into Montana's upper Missouri. A feeling of limitless space is especially powerful during winter, when the blurred whiteness of huge valleys and dozens of mountain ranges in every direction masks the lines of human development.

This austere, barren land is well suited for mountain goats and summering elk, and as refuge for many smaller mammals. It may also be a home for the transitory, endangered gray wolf.

53 Lima Peaks

Immediately northeast of Italian Peaks and separated by only a low-standard road is an 8,237-acre roadless pocket on the edge of Four Eyes Canyon. Grasslands on broad ridges slope gently to steeper, well dissected sidehills with small patches of forest.

The sharp, grassy ridge of the Continental Divide runs east-west through the Red Conglomerate Peaks, forming the 10,000'-high southern boundary of the 42,701-acre Garfield Mountain roadless area. The rounded mounds of the four Lima Peaks rise to the north. Steep, rocky slopes on 10,961' Garfield Mountain tower above a stark, barren land of open grasslands. Isolated stringers of whitebark pine, subalpine fir, lodgepole and juniper cling to the lee sides of ridges and grow in sheltered draws. The north faces of the Lima Peaks are scoured with cirques descending to narrow V-shaped glacial valleys and moraines amidst wide expanses of rolling foothills. Elk calve near the head of Sawmill Creek and summer along the remote Continental Divide. Indian pictographs have been observed along the Middle Fork of Little Sheep Creek.

The best view of the Lima Peaks is from the Forest Service East Creek campground, and the best time is October when the peaks are perfectly framed by the blazing color of aspen.

Total wildlands in Upper Missouri/Great Divide Region: 1,651,300 acres
Amount of designated Wilderness in region: 157,874 acres (9.6%)

Above: Canada geese. **Top:** *Lima Peaks.* **Facing page, top:** *From Eighteenmile Peak, highest point on Montana's Continental Divide.* **Bottom:** *Big Johnson Lake, Anaconda-Pintler Wilderness.*

67

GREATER YELLOWSTONE

LEFT: PAT O'HARA;
BELOW: DENNIS & MARIA HENRY;
RIGHT: ROB OUTLAW

The world's first national park—Yellowstone National Park—may be the single most significant natural area on earth. That it is not an island and cannot be preserved in a vacuum has become widely understood only in the past decade. Greater Yellowstone, which includes major wildlands in Montana north of the park, is the largest essentially-intact ecosystem remaining in the temperate zones of the earth. As the core of the ecosystem, Yellowstone Park gives rise to Montana's premier east-of-the-divide rivers—the Yellowstone, Gallatin and Madison. In turn, these waterways are fed by the undisturbed watersheds of nearly 2½ million acres of wildlands within Montana's share of the Greater Yellowstone Ecosystem.

Above: Fireweed in the Beartooth Wilderness.
Left: Trumpeter swan.
Far left: The Madison Mountains Lakes in Spanish Peaks Wilderness.

69

GREATER YELLOWSTONE

Physiographic region COMPLEX Area Name	Area No.†	Montana Gross Acreage	Agency/ Ownership	Management Status
VI. Greater Yellowstone				
CENTENNIAL MTNS.*	54	50,000	BLM, FS, SEA	ISA, R-NW
RED ROCK LAKES WILDERNESS	55	32,350	FWS	W
SNOWCREST RANGE	56	110,000	FS/BLM/ MDFWP	R-NW, WMA, BLM WSA
GRAVELLY MTNS. COMPLEX	57			
North Gravelly/Axolotl		47,008	BLM, FS	R-NW
Cherry Lakes		12,940	FS	R-NW
Vigilante		16,778	FS	R-NW
Black Butte		39,787	FS	R-NW
Big Horn Mtn.		52,870	FS/MDFWP	R-NW, WMA
Lone Butte		14,138	FS	R-NW
Freezeout Mtn.		95,338	FS	R-NW
EARTHQUAKE (LIONHEAD)*	58	32,780	FS	R-NW
WEST-CENTRAL YELLOWSTONE PLATEAU	59			
South Unit**		17,660	NPS, FS	NP, R-NW
North Unit**		13,000	NPS	NP
MADISON RANGE COMPLEX	60			
Lee Metcalf Wilderness		254,944	FS/BLM	W
Cabin Creek		36,752	FS	RWMA
Cowboys Heaven		26,240	FS	R-NW
Contiguous lands**		35,000	FS/NPS/ BLM	R-NW, NP, MDFWP, WMA
(North Madison: 110,240; South Madison: 242,696)				
GALLATIN RANGE**	61	263,440	FS/NPS/ MDFWP	WAS, NP, WMA, R-NW
ABSAROKA-BEARTOOTH COMPLEX	62			
Absaroka-Beartooth Wild.**		920,310	FS	W
North Absaroka**		238,384	FS/NPS	R-NW, NP
Beartooth		6,320	FS	R-NW
NE Face Beartooth		43,720	FS	R-NW
(Contiguous Absaroka-Beartooth Wildlands: 1,208,734 acres)				
Chico Peak		11,555	FS	R-NW
Reef & Republic Mtn.**		3,000	FS	R-NW
Line Creek Plateau**		20,680	FS	R-NW

Total Wildlands: 2,474,679 acres. Wilderness: 1,207,604 acres (49.0%)

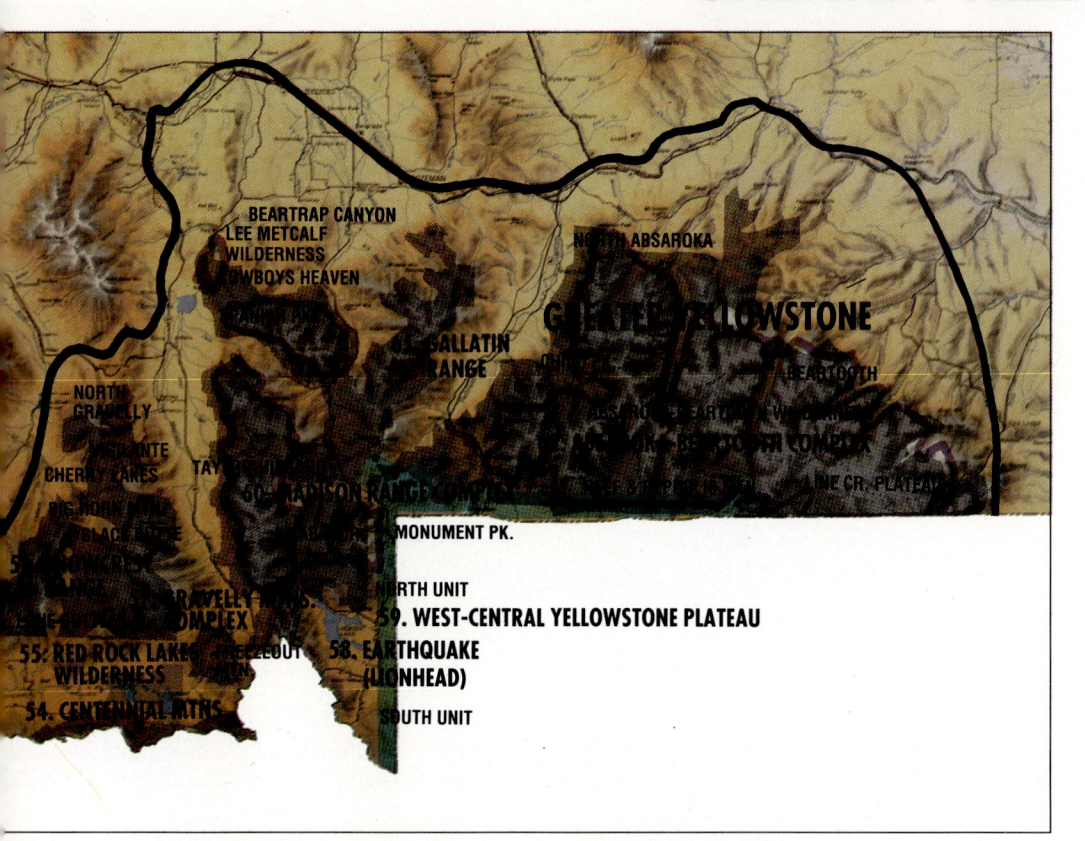

†For identification purposes in this book only
*Areas with contiguous wildlands in Idaho
**Areas with contiguous wildlands in Wyoming

KEY
Agency Symbols
BLM—Bureau of Land Management
FS—Forest Service
FWS—Fish & Wildlife Service
MDFWP—Montana Dept. of Fish, Wildlife & Parks
NPS—National Park Service
P—Private
S—State
SEA—USDA Science & Education Administration
T—Tribal
TNC—The Nature Conservancy

Management Status Symbols
ACEC—BLM Area of Critical Environmental Concern
BLM WSA—Bureau of Land Management Wilderness Study Area
FPA—Forest Service Further Planning Area
ISA—Instant BLM Study Area
NP—National Park
NRA—National Recreation Area
NWR—National Wildlife Refuge
ONA—BLM Outstanding Natural Area
PP—Private Preserve
R-NW—Roadless-Nonwilderness
RWMA—Recreation & Wildlife Management Area
SP—State Park
TPA—Tribal Primitive Area
TR—Tribal Reserve
TW—Tribal Wilderness
W—Wilderness
WMA—State Wildlife Management Area
WSA—Congressional Wilderness Study Area (Forest Service)

54 Centennial Mountains

The Centennials straddle the Continental Divide for 35 miles on the western edge of Greater Yellowstone. The more rugged north slopes in Montana encompass 50,000 acres of wildlands, including a Bureau of Land Management (BLM) Primitive Area recommended for Wilderness designation and the open alpine parks and grasslands of the 16,650-acre U.S. Sheep Experiment Station. The massive upthrust of the range is startling. From an already lofty valley floor of 6,600', this dramatic backdrop to the wetlands of Red Rock Lakes National Wildlife Refuge shoots skyward more than 3,000' in less than one mile.

This divide range is one of the few in the northern Rockies that trend east and west, which may partially explain its rich diversity of native flora and fauna. To date, 362 vascular plant species have been identified in the Centennials. The country is divided by the northeast-trending Odell Creek fault. The core of the higher and steeper eastern Centennials is Precambrian rock overlain by sedimentary rocks. The western Centennials display a variety of earthflows and landslides.

Most wildlife species that were in the range during pristine times are still there, from wintering moose to a large interstate elk herd of 300 to 500 animals. Wolves were sighted as recently as the 1970s and an occasional grizzly bear ambles through high grassy parks, aspen groves and spruce-fir forests in search of a meal. With its prey base on the adjoining Red Rock Lakes refuge, the endangered peregrine falcon nests on protected cliff faces. Here is where we find the source of the Missouri River most distant from its mouth—the headwaters of secluded Hellroaring Creek.

55 Red Rock Lakes Wilderness

Red Rocks is located in the wide-open Centennial Valley. This remote, virtually undeveloped basin, crossed only by gravel roads, holds an amazing system of interconnecting marshes and waterways. More than 14,000 acres of wetlands provide habitat and solitude for a stunning array of birds and other wildlife. The heart of the valley is occupied by the 32,350-acre Red Rock Lakes Wilderness, which comprises about 80 percent of a refuge that was established in 1935 to safeguard the rare trumpeter swan, largest of all North American waterfowl. Some 215 bird species have been observed within this wetlands Wilderness, including 23 kinds of ducks and geese and myriad species of shorebirds, sora rails, eagles and peregrine falcons. The large, shallow Upper and Lower Red Rock lakes are remnants of an ancient and larger lake. Over the millenia the

JOHN REDDY

valley has gradually filled with alluvium. This continuing process will eventually extinguish the lakes. Red Rock Creek still harbors the rare arctic grayling—one of the last native populations outside of Alaska. Moose are year-round residents, but long, snowbound winters send elk, deer and antelope to lower elevations.

56 Snowcrest

As I sat atop the highest summit in the Snowcrest Range—10,581' Sunset Peak—a vast and mostly open landscape spread before me like a big plastic relief map designed to show the shape of the land. Looking along the abrupt west face of the range I could see with one sweeping glance open sagebrush foothills, grassy parks, aspen groves, subalpine meadows, barren talus slopes, forests of Douglas fir and limber pine, gnarled whitebark pine clinging to windswept ridges, all the way up to the matted tundra on the peak. All this within an incredibly short distance.

Perhaps most impressive is the huge East Fork Blacktail Deer Creek basin—a grand mosaic of heavily timbered bottoms, deeply incised streams, rounded grassy knobs and open parks. Glacial features in the Snowcrest are less distinct than in other, more classically glaciated country, due

BILL CUNNINGHAM

Above: Anton Peak, Snowcrest Range.
Top: Red Rock River, Centennial Mountains.

71

to the soft sedimentary rocks that make up most of the range. Rapid weathering of these rocks causes landslides of several hundred acres. The east side is the scarp slope of a north-south trending fault with a shorter, steeper and more dense drainage pattern. The west slope has fewer, flatter streams.

Within these little-known mountains sits a 103,864-acre block of roadless national forest and BLM land. By late fall up to 2,000 elk are migrating west and north to another 50,000 acres of grasslands on the adjacent Blacktail and Robb Creek winter ranges managed by the state and by the Rocky Mountain Elk Foundation. The total contiguous Snowcrest wildland is 110,000 acres.

Here is a place where antelope range to 9,000', where the unearthly call of summering sandhill cranes pierces the mountain air. When hiking this country, you'll have the strange impression of walking in reverse, up out of the mountains onto the plains.

57 Gravelly Mountains Complex

East of the Ruby River, the Gravelly Mountains contain 310,857 acres of mostly open roadless lands fragmented by roads into nine units. However, the Bureau of Land Management's Axolotl Lakes Wilderness Study Area touches both the Sheep Mountain and Crockett Lake roadless areas forming a North Gravelly wildland of 47,008 acres.

This extreme northern end of the range is distinguished by the glacial potholes of Upper Axolotl Lake and Blue Lake, home of a unique form of indigenous tiger salamander. The surrounding country is a transition between lower, open foothills and high hills with mixed conifer forests and meadows. Plentiful elk, a few moose, and some of the highest-elevation antelope habitat in Montana are found here. To the south, broken benches with tree-covered north slopes give way to a broad central grassland. Gentle, grassy benches produce forage of the highest quality, a small amount of which is available to wintering elk and deer.

The tiny Cherry Lakes are pocketed in the upper reaches of 12,940 acres of unroaded deep canyons, sharp breaks and broad grass-sagebrush ridges. Douglas fir, lodgepole pine and aspen stands surround small, wet meadows.

ABOVE: JOHN REDDY; RIGHT: JEFF FOOTT

The main subalpine divide that separates the Ruby and Madison rivers is the head of the 16,778-acre Vigilante roadless area, which drains into the Ruby. A broken series of ridges, steep slopes, and benches are covered about equally with sagebrush/grasses and old-growth Douglas fir and lodgepole sprinkled with aspen and lush meadows.

The 52,870-acre Big Horn Mountain roadless area is centrally located on the east slope and includes the undeveloped portion of the state-managed Wall Creek Wildlife Management Area. This is the most rugged part of the Gravelly, with deep canyons, cliffs, steep benches, undulating basins and high peaks culminating with 10,281' Big Horn Mountain. Forests of Douglas fir and lodgepole dotted with parks give way to unique undisturbed grasslands on Cave Mountain. The southernmost extension of rough fescue grass is found here and on the Wall Creek bench. That bench breaks abruptly into terraces in the Madison Valley. Spelunkers are attracted to Cave Mountain as are elk to calving grounds, winter range and the best hiding cover in the Gravelly Range.

The west slope of the Gravelly Divide includes the 39,787-acre Black Butte roadless area, topped by 10,545' Black Butte—a distinctive landmark rising alone above a sea of subalpine grasslands. Numerous landslides and slumps reflect unstable shale and sandstone soils derived from sedimentary rocks.

The 14,138-acre Lone Butte roadless area is split by the Gravelly Divide on the southern edge of the range overlooking the Centennial Valley. Broad, gently sloping basins along the crest drop to rolling grassy foothills dissected by a dense network of perennial streams.

The 95,338-acre Freezeout Mountain roadless area in the southeast Gravelly is actually divided by a timber sale in the West Fork of the Madison. The larger 65,954-acre block to the northwest encloses moderately steep foothills, broad ridgetops and rolling basins interspersed with rocky canyons in the West Fork Madison and Elk River drainages. Old Indian campsites along the top of the Gravelly Divide overlook the remote, deep canyons of upper Elk River—refuge for some of the last native cutthroat in the Gravelly Range.

The southeast unit of Freezeout Mountain extends from the Cliff Lake Natural Area to the Continental Divide above Antelope Basin. A chain of five lakes sits in a deep, steep-sided rocky canyon cut into adjacent benchlands used by summering elk. The lakes provide nesting habitat for bald eagles and trumpeter swans, with active swan nests on Goose and Elk lakes.

58 Earthquake (Lionhead)

The massive earthquake slide blocking the Madison River on the northwest corner of the 32,780-acre Montana portion of the Lionhead roadless area may foretell of other catastrophic events to come. There is an inherent instability of rocks and soils in these Henry's Lake Mountains, which are actually limestone blocks sitting atop layers of shale and Yellowstone volcanics. The Continental Divide winds for $10^{1}/_{2}$ miles through rolling tundra at the head of four major pristine tributaries to the Madison River. The Lionhead, also dubbed Earthquake, has an unusually high concentration of lofty peaks in a small perimeter along the divide, topped by the area's remote and highest summit, 10,609' Sheep Point. Nine subalpine lakes are tucked away in cirque basins, including the largest and most popular: Coffin Lake. Named for Lionhead Mountain on the Great Divide, this land of dense forests, rock talus and broad mountain parks is where the grizzly walks and where elk and bighorn sheep spend both summer and winter.

59 West-Central Yellowstone Plateau

The only common point shared by Montana, Idaho and Wyoming is where the Continental Divide crosses into Wyoming two miles inside Yellowstone Park. From this juncture north to West Yellowstone, the Montana portion of the undeveloped Madison Plateau comprises 17,660 acres of mostly flat terrain completely covered with lodgepole pine, some of which burned in the gigantic 1988 North Fork Fire. Grizzly bears, elk and deer find security in the dense forests and small canyons.

Another small Montana extension of a vast, wild plateau includes some 13,000 acres in the park, from the Madison River north to Grayling Creek along U.S. Highway 191. Outside of several large wet meadows along Cougar and Duck creeks, the forest cover is almost solid lodgepole. Both of these two-mile-wide roadless strips are part of 2 million acres of recommended Wilderness in Yellowstone Park.

PETE & ALICE BENGEYFIELD

Above: Black Butte in the Gravellies.

Facing page: Lionhead Mountains from the Centennial Valley. Inset: Red fox.

RICHARD FERRIES

Above: *Palisade Falls in the Gallatin Range.*

Facing page: *Hilgard Peak.*

60 Madison Range

The 50-mile-long Madison Range is the westernmost of two fault block massifs running longitudinally from the northwest corner of Yellowstone. The Madisons contain 352,936 roadless acres in north and south units, 254,944 acres of which are designated as the four-part Lee Metcalf Wilderness.

Bear Trap Canyon, our nation's first BLM Wilderness, consists of 6,000 acres of wild canyon country along the Madison River at the northwest terminus of the range. With a maximum depth of 3,000', the steep canyon offers nine miles of possibly the most exciting and challenging whitewater in Montana. Rattlesnakes and moose live along a bottom of sagebrush, scattered shrubs, willow and western cottonwood. From the dry Bear Trap, the ecological bridge of Cowboys Heaven sweeps upward for 6,500' to the crest of the Spanish Peaks. As one of the greatest elevation gains in Montana, this remarkable transition spans the full spectrum of unaltered mountain life zones.

In the Spanish Peaks, glaciers scoured the valleys, changing sharp V-shapes to the present U-shapes, with glacial lakes, knife ridges, near-vertical headwalls and 25 peaks soaring above 10,000', including 11,015' Gallatin Peak. Most of these mountains are made of ancient igneous and sedimentary rocks, converted to gneiss and schist, and they are some of the earth's oldest exposed rocks. The 110,240-acre Bear Trap/Cowboys Heaven/Spanish Peaks wildland is separated from the rest of the range to the south by a development corridor from Jack Creek to Big Sky—the only point where the crest is bisected by a road.

The central and south Madison wild country is a diverse roadless expanse of 242,696 acres made up of the Taylor-Hilgard and Monument Mountain components of the Lee Metcalf Wilderness, the Cabin Creek Recreation and Wildlife Area and contiguous national forest and Yellowstone Park roadless lands.

A vertical mile of glaciated relief imprints the Taylor-Hilgard with jagged peaks, U-shaped valleys and high cirque basins. The smooth sedimentary forms of the Taylor Peaks contrast dramatically with the rugged igneous Hilgard Peaks to the south. Open foothills on the west face of the state's Bear Creek Wildlife Management Area are winter range for more than 500 elk. Some of the prominent landmarks along the crest include the distinctive summits of Sphinx Mountain, the Helmet, Kock Peak and the chimney spires of 11,316' Hilgard Peak—apex of the Madison. About 70 gem-like alpine lakes are nestled along the divide, most of which are in the more rugged southern reaches near Hilgard Peak. Huge grassy subalpine basins and lush meadows spread out across a more subdued landscape in the Skyline Ridge country of Cabin Creek and Monument Mountain. As the only portion of the Wilderness adjacent to Yellowstone, this southeast corner of the Madisons is unexcelled living space for elk, moose and the threatened, free-roaming grizzly.

61 Gallatin Range

Unlike most of Montana's remaining wildlands, which are islands within developed mountain ranges, wildness encompasses almost all of the Gallatin Range. From the Hyalite Peaks just south of Bozeman, 263,440 acres of roadless land extends for 60 miles into the rugged northwest corner of Yellowstone National Park. The national forest portion, which includes a 155,000-acre Montana Wilderness Study Area with some checkerboard private ownership, is the largest unprotected wildland in the Greater Yellowstone Ecosystem. Squeezed between the narrow Gallatin River canyon on the west and the broad Yellowstone River/Paradise Valley to the east, the Gallatins rise to more than 10,000' along an open, often jagged north-south crest.

Picture a mountainscape first formed by compression and later covered by lava from the Yellowstone volcanic field and you're looking at the Gallatin. Some 6,000' of layered andesite, breccia and conglomerate built the volcanic mound that is today the long, arching ridge of Hyalite Peaks, named for a locally abundant colorless opal.

The vast Gallatin Petrified Forest near Specimen Ridge along the heads of Tom Miner, Rock, Porcupine and Buffalo Horn creeks presents a rare look at trees that were petrified in their original growing positions. The living forest is also worthy of note. Broad open slopes are dominated by big sage, with their northern exposures

74

PAT O'HARA

WILDLANDS AND WILDLIFE

RON SANFORD

Elk cow.

Montana is the envy of the hunting public, with its six-week general rifle season, over-the-counter elk tags and astounding variety of big-game species. But as one who well remembers when seasons and bag limits were far more liberal, I look with alarm at a clock that continues to tick on the relative freedoms enjoyed by sportsmen and sportswomen in Montana. As wildland melts like the proverbial snowbank in June, additional restrictions and regulations substitute as wildlife security. If the old-growth thickets that once hid elk are clearcut, the compensation for this reduced natural security comes to us as reduced hunting opportunities. A computer randomly spitting out limited permits takes the place of what was once roadless, wild and remote.

Big bulls with regal racks have a chance to grow old in unroaded expanses where protection comes from dark ancient forests, doghair lodgepole pine, steep slopes and hidden canyons without trails or names. The preservation and pursuit of wildlife has a special quality when the land that produces and protects the animal likewise is wild. Without this security the dignity of the hunt is compromised, the game more vulnerable. It follows that the pursuit of the animal—hunting—becomes vulnerable as well. To paraphrase the National Rifle Association, which has often opposed Wilderness, "you can take my Wilderness out of my cold, dead fingers." For as wildlands go, so goes the sport hunting of wildlife.

Right or wrong, game animals are more favored than species we regard as "competitors" or "threats." In reality, a rich and diverse mosaic of all species—mammals, fish, birds, reptiles and insects—is crucial to wilderness ecosystems. Some big carnivores, such as the grizzly and wolf, require the large, unmodified habitat of wilderness to survive, and are thus wilderness-dependent. Because they are at the top of the food chain, their condition tells us how other species lower on the food chain are doing. Herbivores, notably elk and deer, thrive in early- to mid-successional stages of vegetation. In the absence of fire, wildlife would reach high population levels for a brief period followed by many years of lower densities as the forest moves toward "climax." A mosaic of plant communities supports the greatest diversity of wildlife. Fire in wilderness can restore and maintain this mosaic if allowed to operate.

Whether we pursue wildlife with weapon, camera, or our dreams, the chance to view animals in their natural, native surroundings is a vital part of what we consider to be a wilderness experience. Wildlife and wildlands are inseparable—one cannot be diminished without diminishing the other, either in quantity or quality.

typically covered by dense forests of Douglas fir, aspen, spruce and lodgepole. Tundra, turf and rock adorn the crest where the wind roars like a runaway freight train.

The southern Gallatin is exceptional grizzly country as well as some of the finest elk range anywhere, with its blend of open grassland forage and dense forest hiding cover. Two bighorn sheep herds of about 150 animals each live here with another smaller band in the Hyalite Peaks. Along with a stunning assemblage of wild creatures, an almost unnerving volcanic geology lends mystique to this island atop a maddened hot spot.

62 Absaroka-Beartooth Wildlands

On the northeast side of Yellowstone rises the enormous uplift of the Absaroka and Beartooth ranges, one of the highest, wildest and most austere alpine expanses on the continent. For 65 miles across its widest, southern boundary, only a couple of short low-standard roads penetrate these mountains. The north-flowing Boulder River is born in the high country and is the dividing line between the Absaroka Range on the west and the Beartooth Mountains to the east. With a unified Wilderness core of 920,310 acres in Montana, the Absaroka-Beartooth encompasses the second largest contiguous roadless area in the state—1,208,734 acres, which includes the northeast edge of Yellowstone Park.

The Beartooth Range, named after a sharp point jutting from the jaw of Beartooth Mountain, contains 29 peaks above 12,000' and culminates in Montana's highest and wildest mountain—12,799' Granite Peak. The names of nearby summits describe the mood of this harsh moonscape: Froze-to-Death, Tempest, Thunder. Lofty tundra plateaus form the largest contiguous land mass above 10,000' in the United States. The range is derived from a Precambrian base that, at 4 billion years, is among the oldest known rock in the world. This foundation was covered with thousands of feet of sediments and then uplifted 70 million years ago. Thick ice scoured the southern side of the Beartooth Plateau, leaving rolling topography. The highest peaks are islands of sedimentary rock that escaped the ice. On the northern flank the ice carved out U-shaped valleys and created the distinct, alternating plateau-canyon landscape. With an astounding 386 plant species discovered thus far, the Beartooth displays a flora richer than any other mountain range in North America. Perhaps this is due to the tremendous height of the range in combination with its unusual east-west orientation.

A profusion of water in all its forms is the overriding impression of the Absaroka-Beartooth. Three-hundred-foot waterfalls plummeting to snowbound cirque lakes; countless cascades and nearly 1,000 deep-blue lakes remind us that these wild mountains are an undisturbed watershed for our nation's longest undammed river—the free-flowing Yellowstone.

In contrast to the Beartooths, the Absaroka Range is made of softer sedimentary rock that has eroded into gentler, more rounded mountains. Exceptions exist, such as jagged Mount Cowan with its ring of spires. The southern portion of the range is especially productive for grizzly bears, moose, bighorn sheep and summering elk and deer. It is common to spot soaring golden eagles—swept by the wind and bathed in mountain light.

Because of moist micro-climates, foothills and canyons along the northwest face of the Absarokas nurture plants unusual east of Montana's Continental Divide, such as beargrass, rare ferns and the state's only population of high-bush cranberry. Grassy foothills dotted with aspen along the north face of the range provide winter range for elk, deer and bighorn sheep.

RICK GRAETZ

The Absaroka-Beartooth Wilderness is characterized by the profusion of water. Here, Sky Top Lakes Basin.

77

On the extreme west side of the Absarokas overlooking the Paradise Valley is the 11,555-acre Chico Peak roadless area, dominated by its 10,195' namesake mountain. The northern slopes of the roadless area are heavily forested with lodgepole and Douglas fir with some bighorn sheep summer and winter grounds near Green Mountain. High rocky ridges and alpine meadows radiate southward from Chico Peak.

Just south of Cooke City, two small roadless extensions into Montana—totaling 3,000 acres—are contiguous to the North Absaroka Wilderness in Wyoming. The rugged north slopes of Republic Mountain are marked by cliffs, talus, steep ravines and spur ridges. A high rough ridge gives the Reef its name, as it rises in a series of scarps to above 10,000' just north of imposing Pilot Peak. The lower, gentler slopes of Woody Ridge are used by wandering grizzlies and wintering wildlife.

The scenic southern backdrop to Red Lodge is Line Creek Plateau—an extension of the eastern flanks of the Beartooth. The northern 20,680 acres of this large interstate roadless area reach into Montana. A diverse land of abrupt canyons, lower-elevation forests and treeless tundra provides a mix of summer and winter habitat for elk, mule deer, bighorn sheep, mountain goats and blue grouse. A unique organic horizon of fibrous turf and limestone bedrock in this dry alpine ecosystem sustains more than 20 rare species of plants, some of which are known to grow in only one or two locations in the west.

Total Wildlands in Greater Yellowstone Region:
    2,474,679 acres
Total Amount of Designated Wilderness: 1,207,604 (49%)

Balsamroot and a view of Elephanthead Peak in the Absaroka Mountains.

DOES WILDERNESS HAVE A RIGHT TO ITS WATER?

JOHN REDDY

Hyalite Creek in the Gallatin Mountains.

All the values we associate with wilderness arise from water, wild and free as the land it drains from the time it falls as a snowflake along a remote divide to when it tumbles madly through an untamed canyon. The specter of waterless wilderness is almost unimaginable. We've complacently assumed that wild land and wild water never would be separated. After all, most of our existing and proposed wilderness is headwaters country, high above the agricultural uses that account for about 97 percent of Montana's water consumption. But, with growing competition for scarce water, the wilderness wars of the 1980s may pale in comparison to the water wars of the '90s. Designation of Wilderness by itself may not be enough to safeguard its life-giving water. For example, a downstream water user with prior rights could move the point of diversion upstream within a wilderness boundary. Future Montana wilderness legislation must contain water rights language asserting a federally reserved water right to fulfill the preservation purposes for which the wilderness is designated. The challenge is to cooperatively craft wilderness water rights language for Montana that will protect wilderness as well as valid existing water rights. Wilderness will not be truly secure until this is accomplished.

MANAGEMENT FROM THE GROUND UP

Gone are the days of simply drawing a boundary around a Wilderness Area and leaving it alone. "Wilderness management," which at first glance seems like an inherent contradiction in terms, has evolved during the past quarter century in response to growing numbers of visitors who expect quality when they enter Wilderness.

Since 1905, the Forest Service itself has evolved with a policy of confrontation and accommodation. The pattern goes like this. An interest group applies pressure on the agency. In order to protect its autonomy, the Forest Service stimulates counter-pressure from an opposing interest group. Once comfortably "in the middle," the claim is made that "we must be doing something right since no one likes what we're doing." The ensuing accommodation of the use at hand causes resource damage in the form of silted streams, visual blight and loss of wildlife habitat.

The Wilderness system has been managed in much the same way, from benign neglect to outright accommodation of incompatible uses, such as allowing outfitter caches in the Frank Church-River of No Return Wilderness of central Idaho. Even the Forest Service admits that wilderness conditions have gone downhill. University of Montana Forestry Dean Emeritus Arnold Bolle is adamant that accommodation is not acceptable in wilderness.

As our nation's most distinguished forester, Dr. Bolle has helped pioneer a more enlightened approach to wilderness management in the Bob Marshall Wilderness, called Limits of Acceptable Change (LAC). The basic idea is to get all of the interested parties together for open discussion without a preconceived plan or bias. Early on, the Bob Marshall LAC group agreed on a common goal, as established in the Wilderness Act, to protect an enduring wilderness resource. When it comes to this goal "there can be no give, no accommodation," stresses Bolle. Interestingly, because of its tendency to accommodate, the Forest Service was at first less committed to the enduring wilderness goal than were the users.

Ultimately, the group identified four broad opportunity classes in the Bob, ranging from pristine class 1—with no trails and a high degree of solitude—to class 4, where more encounters with people are expected. Despite this practical recognition of varying levels of use, there are no sacrifice areas. The basic goal applies throughout the Wilderness. Arnold Bolle sees LAC as "real public involvement," from setting the major goal to monitoring to implementation, because everyone in the group is a "fellow learner" who must first agree on what the problems are before plunging into solutions. Monitoring conditions and changes makes LAC a continuing process, but this vital step is only about 30 percent funded. Bolle suggests that the Forest Service make up the shortfall from its timber budget.

Dr. Bolle criticizes the Forest Service for taking "unholy advantage" of dedicated young wilderness rangers who are underpaid and without career incentives. Thus far, the localized impacts of overuse and abuse within the Wilderness are more sociological than ecological. Still, Bolle stresses that knowledge of ecosystems and long-term trends is more necessary in wilderness than anywhere else.

The present system of management has allowed quality to deteriorate by basing success on the increased quantity of users. Bolle advises Forest Service managers to "get quality into your minds, onto the land, and only then into the memos and handbooks."

Dr. Bolle partly attributes the open warfare between the Forest Service and citizen groups over wildland allocation to the agency's attitude that acres in the Wilderness System are "lost." The LAC process, which demands honesty from all of its participants, can be a way out of this quagmire. Honest management would involve changing people's behavior through education to meet the overriding goal of enduring wilderness.

But the funding and commitment for honest, high-quality wilderness management are not going to happen until the public demands them. This is where folks like retired Region One Director of Recreation and Lands Bill Worf of Stevensville come in. Worf is nationally respected as an unwavering watchdog of the Wilderness System.

Although he has a reputation as a "purist" in wilderness management, he prefers being called a "strict constructionist" of the Wilderness Act. In his view there should be no deliberate, avoidable, human-caused impacts in wilderness. To develop public support for management of this quality Worf has co-founded Wilderness Watch, a national citizen group focusing on management rather than allocation. Worf warns that "if we don't pay attention to management, 20 years from now the system won't be worth saving."

JOHN REDDY

Fred King and Arnold Foss of the Montana Department of Fish, Wildlife and Parks.

WILD ISLANDS IN THE PRAIRIE

FACING PAGE: TOM DIETRICH;
BELOW AND RIGHT: JOHN REDDY

*I*n Montana's central and north-central heartland, the valleys are so broad that the isolated mountain ranges seem like islands in an endless prairie sea. And within these islands are vestiges of wildness seemingly intensified by the vastness of their uncluttered surroundings. Across this great semi-arid space rise the Sweetgrass Hills, Bearpaws, Highwoods, Big and Little Belts, Elkhorns, Castles and Big Snowies. On the south end the Shields River Valley separates the Bridgers and the Crazies, Montana's most impressive islands of montane habitat.

Above: *On the Smith River.*
Left: *Big Belt Mountains.*

Facing page: *Wheat fields and the Highwood Mountains near Danvers.*

81

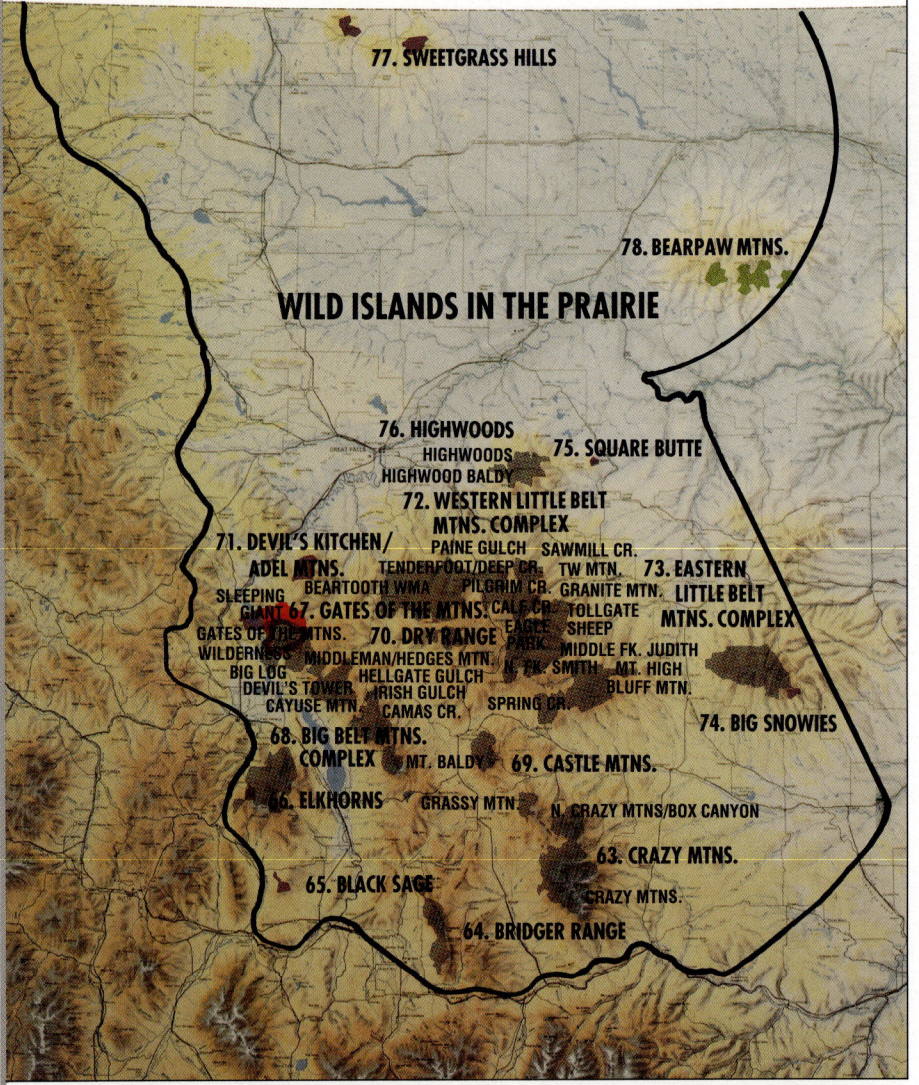

WILD ISLANDS IN THE PRAIRIE

† For identification purposes in this book only
* Areas with contiguous wildlands in Idaho
** Areas with contiguous wildlands in Wyoming

KEY
Agency Symbols
BLM—Bureau of Land Management
FS—Forest Service
FWS—Fish & Wildlife Service
MDFWP—Montana Dept. of Fish, Wildlife & Parks
NPS—National Park Service
P—Private
S—State
SEA—USDA Science & Education Administration
T—Tribal
TNC—The Nature Conservancy

Management Status Symbols
ACEC—BLM Area of Critical Environmental Concern
BLM WSA—Bureau of Land Management Wilderness Study Area
FPA—Forest Service Further Planning Area
ISA—Instant BLM Study Area
NP—National Park
NRA—National Recreation Area
NWR—National Wildlife Refuge
ONA—BLM Outstanding Natural Area
PP—Private Preserve
R-NW—Roadless-Nonwilderness
RWMA—Recreation & Wildlife Management Area
SP—State Park
TPA—Tribal Primitive Area
TR—Tribal Reserve
TW—Tribal Wilderness
W—Wilderness
WMA—State Wildlife Management Area
WSA—Congressional Wilderness Study Area (Forest Service)

Physiographic region Complex Area Name	Area No.†	Montana Gross Acreage	Agency/ Ownership	Management Status
VII. Wild Islands in the Prairie				
Crazy Mtns. Complex	63			
Crazy Mtns.		136,547	FS	R-NW
N. Crazy Mtns./Box Canyon		12,920	FS	R-NW
Bridger Range	64	47,512	FS	R-NW
Black Sage	65	5,926	BLM	R-NW, BLM WSA
Elkhorns	66	89,585	FS/BLM	WMA, R-NW
Gates of the Mountains Complex	67			
Gates of the Mtns. Wild.		28,562	FS	W
Big Log addition		12,045	FS	R-NW
Sleeping Giant		10,414	BLM	ACEC
Beartooth WMA		29,000	MDFWP	WMA
(Contiguous Gates of the Mountains Wildlands: 69,607)				
Big Belt Mtns. Complex	68			
Devil's Tower		7,200	FS	R-NW
Middleman/Hedges Mtn.		34,250	FS	R-NW
Hellgate Gulch		18,430	FS	R-NW
Cayuse Mtn.		19,353	FS	R-NW
Irish Gulch		7,787	FS	R-NW
Camas Creek		28,832	FS	R-NW
Mt. Baldy		18,700	FS	R-NW
Grassy Mtn.		6,453	FS	R-NW
Castle Mtns.	69	29,900	FS	R-NW
The Dry Range	70	14,605	FS/P	R-NW
Devil's Kitchen/Adel Mtns.	71	19,069	BLM/P	R-NW
Western Little Belt Mtns. Complex/ Smith River	72			
Tenderfoot/Deep Creek		98,500	FS	R-NW
Pilgrim Creek		50,000	FS	R-NW
Calf Creek		11,020	FS	R-NW
Eagle Park		6,300	FS	R-NW
Eastern Little Belt Mtns. Complex	73			
Paine Gulch		8,500	FS	R-NW
Sawmill Creek		12,800	FS	R-NW
TW Mtn.		8,800	FS	R-NW
Big Baldy		44,200	FS	R-NW
Granite Mtn.		10,580	FS	R-NW
Tollgate-Sheep		27,000	FS	R-NW
Middle Fork Judith		92,145	FS	WSA
N. Fork Smith		8,800	FS	R-NW
Mt. High		33,000	FS	R-NW
Bluff Mtn.		37,120	FS	R-NW
Spring Creek		19,800	FS	R-NW
Big Snowies	74	104,755	FS/BLM	WSA, R-NW, BLM WSA
Square Butte	75	1,947	BLM	ISA, ONA
Highwoods	76			
Highwood Baldy		15,600	FS	R-NW
Highwoods		24,300	FS	R-NW
Sweetgrass Hills	77	6,957	BLM	ACEC
Bearpaw Mtns.	78	50,000	T, P	R-NW

Total Wildlands: 1,249,214 acres. Wilderness: 28,562 acres (2.3%)

63 Crazy Mountains

From the low terraces of the Yellowstone to the jagged summit of 11,214' Crazy Peak, the country rises more than 7,000' in what is perhaps the most startling transition from prairie to mountains in Montana. The stark shapes of 23 rugged peaks top 10,000', bearing the signatures of extensive glaciation that forced these crags in different directions simultaneously. Legend has it that a white woman driven crazy when Indians killed her family wandered into the mountains to haunt the Indians. But a topographical explanation for the range's name is its convoluted geological formations. They comprise one of the largest exposed blocks of igneous rock in the world.

Volcanic in origin, the core of the higher southern Crazy Mountains is a vast igneous intrusion from which spectacular swarms of wall-like dikes radiate, some of which are more than 50' thick. As one of the few central Montana montane islands high enough to support large glaciers during the last Ice Age, the Crazies are a maze of nearly vertical peaks, sawtooth ridges, arêtes, talus fields at the base of broken cliffs, and lush alpine cirque basins with 40 snow-fed lakes.

On cross-country treks I've been amazed to find mountain goats on ridges and sideslopes seemingly barren of all plant life except rock-hugging lichens. To the north, the range becomes lower and gentler, breaking into groups of forested hills and canyons that drain into the Musselshell. Tortuous terrain has kept a 136,547-acre core of this oval uplift pristine despite checkerboard inholdings dating from the 1865 Northern Pacific land grants.

In 1857, Plenty Coups, the last great pre-reservation chief of the Crow Indians, realized a vision on top of Crazy Peak with which to guide his people. The continued wildness of these sacred mountains inspires modern-day members of his tribe to practice traditional religion here—from purification in lakeside sweat lodges to vision quests on lofty pinnacles above the prairie.

The northwest corner of the Crazies holds the 12,920-acre Box Canyon roadless area, which consists mainly of a broad, open north-south ridge with deep canyons on both sides. The contrast of sagebrush-grass on south slopes and stringers of Douglas fir and lodgepole pine on north aspects provides elk with valuable winter range.

64 Bridger Range

Across the Shields Valley west of the Crazies, the Bridger Mountains form Bozeman's scenic backdrop on the north. Most of the range is occupied by a 47,512-acre roadless area, which is split in the north by a road and powerline through Flathead Pass. The uplifted fault blocks of heavily glaciated peaks are strewn with sedimentary rock. From a distance, the most distinctive landmarks in the long, narrow uplift are its highest point—9,670' Sacajawea Peak—and the 9,004' limestone tower of Ross Peak. Steep forested slopes grade into alpine tundra where at least 60 mountain goats climb high rocky ridges. Native herds of elk and mule deer along with moose descend to winter ranges along the western foothills.

65 Black Sage

Rolling hills ranging between 5,000' and 6,000' rise just east of the Boulder River in the 5,926-acre Black Sage Bureau of Land Management Wilderness Study Area. Nearly half of this irregularly shaped dry country is covered with juniper, mountain mahogany and limber pine, with Douglas fir on the protected north and east slopes. The forested face of a centrally-located limestone ridge is the most dominant feature. Natural diversity is low because of narrow elevational differences. Still, these undeveloped sage-covered hills offer exceptional spring-winter habitat for plentiful mule deer and spring-summer range for a smaller herd of antelope.

ABOVE: DAVID MATHERLY; TOP: DENNIS J. CWIDAK

Above: *Crevasse in the Crazy Mountains.*
Top: *Autumn tranquility in the Crazies.*

BILL CUNNINGHAM

North end of the Elkhorn Mountains from Casey Peak.

66 The Elkhorns

Within the 175,700-acre Elkhorns Wildlife Management Area just southeast of Helena lies an essentially roadless, wild core of 89,585 acres. The range is a vast, uplifted block defined by major faults on the north, east and south. The Elkhorns rise 1,000' to 2,000' above and east of the Continental Divide, thereby picking up considerably more moisture from prevailing storms than do the lower, surrounding mountains.

The range is made up of three distinct sub-regions. First, the high Elkhorn/Crow Peaks complex ascends to 9,400' in the southern end providing panoramic vistas, alpine lakes and rugged topography formed when ancient glaciers carved striking rock walls at the head of Tizer Creek. To the north is the expansive Tizer Basin, with abundant lodgepole-pine/subalpine-fir/spruce forests, small clearings, primitive jeep trails, old mining structures and large grassy meadows. Thirdly, the upper reaches of McClellan and Beaver creeks enclose the most primitive portion of the Elkhorns with dense young trees, high rocky ridges and deep canyons. Much of this secluded north end burned in the huge 1988 Warm Springs fire.

The lushness and wide elevation changes in these mountains account for the amazing array of 148 known species of mammals, birds, amphibians and reptiles. With an abundance of eight of Montana's big-game animals the Elkhorns are among Montana's most productive and heavily-hunted elk areas. Unlike most other elk habitat in the state, about 80 percent of the winter range is publicly owned.

The jury is still out on the question of whether the Forest Service can manage a large block of national forest with wildlife as the number one priority without the added protection of designated Wilderness. In the face of growing pressure for mineral exploration, the long-term commitment of the agency will surely be revealed by its decisions in the Elkhorns.

67 Gates of the Mountains Wildlands Complex

When Lewis and Clark first entered the Rocky Mountains, it seemed as though the immense limestone cliffs along the Missouri River would block their passage. Suddenly, the river twisted through a narrow "Gates of the Mountains" canyon. Hence the name of a compact 28,562-acre Wilderness which is the core of 70,000 acres of diverse wildlands in the northern Big Belts.

West of the Missouri the Sleeping Giant landform, officially known as 6,792' Beartooth Mountain, resembles a huge fellow on his back with his feet toward the Continental Divide and the distinctive profile of his craggy face toward the Gates of the Mountains. The giant's great barrel chest is open native grassland with slow-growing ponderosa pine, limber pine and Douglas fir draping his sides and the lower ridges that form his arms. Mountain goats climb the giant's massive nose and other facial features which are the "bear teeth" of vertical rock outcroppings. Bighorn sheep are found within this dry, geologically unusual 10,414-acre Bureau of Land Management Area of Critical Environmental Concern.

In the Gates of the Mountains Wilderness and surrounding wildlands the effects of 300 million years of erosion on sedimentary rock beds have left an intriguing landscape of sheer cliffs, shallow caves, spires and pinnacles. Dramatic folding and faulting of the limestone exposes fossil beds where animal and plant remains from the Mississippian period have been preserved in the finest detail. The jagged terrain of plunging canyons and bold knife ridges contrasts with higher-elevation parks where the country smoothes into sloping meadows and open bald ridges. A rough-hewn character is imparted to the land by the scars of large fires, such as the disastrous Mann Gulch fire of 1949 and the 1984 North Hills fire.

Osprey are common along the Missouri, as are sure-footed goats on the rugged cliffs above the river. Bighorn sheep were successfully transplanted to the adjacent Beartooth Wildlife Management Area—an undeveloped expanse of winter range and deep canyons a bit larger than the Wilderness. With a herd of more than 300 it is not unusual to see 20 to 30 mature rams on the secluded slopes of massive 7,980' Moors Mountain during July.

68 Big Belt Mountains Wildlands Complex

From Beaver Creek southeast to Grassy Mountain, the Big Belts are riddled with roads and off-road-vehicle playgrounds. Still, rugged terrain maintains wildness in eight roadless areas totaling 141,005 acres. Bordering the junction of Beaver Creek with the Missouri River is a 7,200-acre roadless tract of dry, rolling hills surrounding 5,090' Devil's Tower. With gentle foothills leading to a rocky, deeply dissected interior, most of the area is important winter range for elk and mule deer.

In 1981 floodwaters took out part of the Trout Creek

road that divided Middleman Mountain-Hedges Mountain, thereby uniting this 34,250-acre roadless area along the southwest slopes of the Big Belts. Gentle foothills with rounded ridges rise to sheer cliffs and knife ridges where mountain goats roam. A popular national recreation trail climbs into Hanging Valley, which is encircled by a thick forest of Douglas fir and lodgepole.

The second largest panel of pictographs discovered in Montana is near the mouth of Hellgate Gulch on the lower edge of an 18,430-acre roadless area. Arrowheads and scrapers are scattered throughout these gnarled cliffs and gently rolling uplands. Elk and mule deer winter along an abrupt transition from dry grassland to dense forest.

The 19,353-acre Cayuse Mountain roadless area is a long, narrow series of steep slopes, tight draws and high buttes wedged between White and Avalanche gulches. Elk and mule deer find winter feed on dry south-facing hills dotted with rock outcrops, open Douglas fir and fescue grasses. Prehistoric Indian camps have been found in tiny parks below the many twisting feeder ridges that lead to the main divide.

The Belt Mountain Divide forms the head of Irish Gulch in a 7,787-acre roadless pocket of dry, lower ridges leading up to thick forests of lodgepole pine and Douglas fir. Thomas Gulch provides some of the best elk and deer winter range in the Big Belts. Willow bottoms attract a few moose year-round.

The high Big Belt Divide climbs to the exposed, rock-strewn 8,942' summit of Boulder Baldy in the heart of the 28,832-acre Camas Creek roadless area north of Duck Creek Pass. This wildland is a jumble of open parks, sheer cliffs, rock slides, intimate streams and steep-sided forested valleys. Glacial cirques carved into the central divide hide remote trout-filled lakes framed with rocks, cliffs and a border of lodgepole, spruce and fir. As the often-steep divide flattens in places, wide expanses of whitebark pine appear. Mountain goats find refuge along secluded cliffs, as do plentiful elk in the cover of dense forests on the east slope.

South of Duck Creek Pass, the Big Belts attain monumental proportions as they stretch a vertical mile from the Missouri River to over 9,400' atop Mt. Baldy and Mt. Edith. More than 80 percent of the lofty 18,700-acre Mt. Baldy roadless area rises above 7,000', giving the country a distinctively alpine flavor. The main divide wraps around the north-facing Birch Creek basin, a vast glacial cirque holding a dozen jewel-like lakes. On the north edge of the basin a series of jagged granite spires known as the Needles guard an open meadow enclosed by lodgepole pine with hidden elk wallows. Once, while roaming the open tundra plateaus of the Baldy-Edith ridge in early fall, I encountered a dozen mountain goats in a high saddle. Like an apparition they vanished instantly into the mountain mist. Continuing east, I witnessed a golden eagle migration of at least 100 of the great birds of prey circling over the rock-strewn tundra plateau of Mt. Edith.

The Big Belt Divide forms the upper reaches of the 6,453-acre wedge-shaped Grassy Mountain roadless area in the southeast corner of the range. Elk and mule deer summer in small parks below timberline on up to open sagebrush grasslands along the 7,000' crest. Densely-forested slopes drop steeply into Cedar Bar and Carl creeks, connected to each other by trail.

69 Castle Mountains

Formed by granite intrusion, the west end of the igneous Castles are lush and moist—unlike the dry, porous limestone mountains of the adjacent east Castles and Little Belts. The top of centrally-located 8,552' Wapiti Peak affords a commanding view of most of the 29,900-acre Castle Mountains roadless area and, on a clear day, of the Sweetgrass Hills on the distant Canadian border. "Castle turrets" of 50-foot-high igneous spires adorn the west slopes. Higher elevations are dominated by a central cluster of peaks above 8,000', holding expansive parks of several square miles surrounded by lodgepole and limber pine. Primitive trails from the early mining days wind through a blend of meadows and dark, nearly impenetrable forest ideal for the wily wapiti.

JOHN REDDY

Gates of the Mountains Wilderness near York.

Middle Fork of the Judith River.

70 The Dry Range

Most of the Dry Range between the Big and Little Belts lies within the 14,605-acre Ellis Canyon roadless area, which meets the Smith River near Rock Creek. The Dry Range is intermingled with alternate sections of national forest, some of which may be traded for private land in the popular Smith River corridor. Ellis Canyon, with its steep limestone sides, is the most prominent feature. Scattered ponderosa pines grow on the canyon faces that ascend to gentle grassland parks and ridgetops marked with limber pine and rock outcrops. Prehistoric Indians left arrowheads around springs, along with fire scars and pictographs on the walls of limestone caves.

71 Devil's Kitchen—Adel Mountains

The Adel Mountains immediately southeast of the Missouri River near Craig are known for laccoliths—volcanic buttes with flat tops. Lesser known is Devil's Kitchen—a rugged, wild core of 19,069 acres. Devil's Kitchen itself is a network of steep, open ridges and dry canyons dropping more than 1,000' into Cox Creek from timbered plateaus and hillsides. Roughly 70 million years ago, thick sections of volcanic rock erupted over Cretaceous sandstones and mudstones. Gentle and more densely forested in the south, the country becomes more open, steep and rugged in the central section from Devil's Kitchen to the South Fork of Sheep Creek, changing back to thick forest on the north end around Harris Mountain. The Sawteeth, an aptly named series of cliffs at the head of the South Fork of Sheep Creek, are favored by mountain goats and bighorn sheep. The rough-hewn Adels are lightly visited due to the checkerboard ownership pattern of Bureau of Land Management and private land.

72 Western Little Belts Wildlands Complex

The million-acre expanse of the relatively gentle Little Belt Range sprawls eastward for 70 miles from the Smith River to Judith Gap. Despite a spaghetti-like network of logging roads, nearly half of these forested uplands remain wild in 15 roadless tracts. Highway 89 bisects the range over King's Hill, forming a line between the western and eastern portions of the range.

As the largest chunk of roadless country in the Little Belts, the 98,500-acre Tenderfoot-Deep Creek area has 25 miles of the wild Smith River as its western boundary. The 61-mile stretch of the Smith from Camp Baker to Eden Bridge is Montana's premier overnight float, with 400'-high limestone walls, a gentle gradient of S-curves, and good fishing for rainbow and brown trout. The deepest, most awe-inspiring canyons envelop the river from Tenderfoot Creek north and downstream to Deep Creek. Other attractions include the 25-mile Deep Creek loop national recreation trail, a series of 20' to 30' waterfalls on Tenderfoot Creek and a mosaic of large meadows and dense forests well suited for elk, deer, moose and black bear. Tipi rings, pictographs, tools and arrowheads along the Smith conjure images of prehistoric Indians hunting, camping and traveling along the river.

The circular 50,000-acre Pilgrim Creek roadless area lies along the northwest edge of the Little Belts. The entire Pilgrim Creek drainage is enclosed within its namesake roadless area, which rises to a central dome formed by Thunder Mountain and 7,670' Big Horn Mountain. These subalpine summits of rock, scree and whitebark pine drop a couple thousand feet to moderately steep canyons with limestone cliffs that stand above lower Pilgrim Creek where it enters Belt Creek. Upper Pilgrim Creek and Thunder Mountain are often used by a small elk herd.

Elk are also attracted to a broad park at the head of Calf Creek in an 11,020-acre roadless area in the southwest corner of the Little Belts. These gently rolling parklands drop southward to timbered ridges and flat, open U-shaped canyon bottoms where aspens lend diversity to the adjacent forest of lodgepole and Douglas fir.

The 6,300-acre Eagle Park roadless area of mostly gentle but heavily forested foothills forms a three- to four-mile transition from the prairie to the mountains. Eagle Creek begins as a sharp V-shape below open parks, becoming more U-shaped lower down where elk winter on grassy benches.

73 Eastern Little Belts Wildlands Complex

The 8,500-acre Paine Gulch roadless area in the north-central Little Belts is bordered on the west by U.S. 89—the only winter access across the range. Paine Gulch itself is a rectangular box canyon formed by steep, parallel 6,500' ridges and 7,230' Servoss Mountain on the south. The country is dry and weathered with almost no undergrowth beneath scattered Douglas fir and ponderosa pine. Ecological processes are running their natural course in undisturbed habitats representative of the Lewis and Clark

National Forest. Therefore, forest managers have selected the west half of Paine Gulch as a research natural area.

The adjacent 12,800-acre Sawmill Creek roadless area to the northeast is dominated by 8,309' Barker Mountain—a dome-shaped laccolith. Like spokes on a wheel, Barker's rounded ridges fan out in all directions. Natural openings break up an otherwise continuous forest of Douglas fir, lodgepole and limber pine.

Mountains meet the plains along the northern boundary of the 8,800-acre TW Mountain roadless area. An open north-south ridgeline of nearly 8,000' connects three prominent mountains to form an east-facing bowl that flattens into Lone Tree Park.

At 9,175', Big Baldy Mountain is the highest point in the Little Belts. It is also the centerpiece of its namesake 44,200-acre roadless area in the north end of the range. Glaciers carved three lake-filled cirques into the southeast face of this massive mountain. The surrounding ridges, sidehills and creek bottoms are a mix of lodgepole pine, Douglas fir and sparse undergrowth typical of the Little Belts. Big grassy parks coveted by summering elk drape over high ridges with small, intimate openings scattered throughout the lower-elevation forest.

The slopes of the 10,580-acre Granite Mountain roadless area gradually climb to around 7,700' atop Granite and Taylor peaks in the northeast corner of the Little Belts. Interestingly, Wolf Butte—1,000' lower and looking much like a wolf's tooth—is the most prominent landmark. The butte can be seen from as far away as Great Falls—50 miles northwest—because of its location and distinctive shape. A large cave on the northwest side of Granite overlooks the Hellhole—where cliff walls drop sharply from the sides of Taylor and Granite mountains.

The northeast Little Belts contain the irregularly-shaped 27,000-acre Tollgate-Sheep roadless area, which wraps around five prominent peaks approaching 8,000'. Of these only Bandbox Mountain rises above timberline. Bandbox is noted for fossils, including an ancient coral reef formation. The southeast corner of the roadless area adjoins the state-managed Judith River Wildlife Management Area, which winters some 1,200 elk.

The heart of the eastern Little Belts is the 92,145-acre Middle Fork Judith—one of only two Montana Wilderness Study Act Areas east of the main range of the Rockies. This circular pocket of wild elk country stretches east for 17 miles from the striking headwall basins of the Middle and Lost Forks to lower foothills and canyons, with a north-south extent of 13 miles. Broad, moderately rolling ridges rise above blankets of elk-hiding lodgepole interspersed with limestone outcrops and grassy parks. The Middle Fork Judith is the only year-round stream flowing east from the Little Belts. A small pure-strain population of cutthroat trout survives in the upper Lost Fork despite a high natural silt load. Roadless security and good habitat combine to make the Middle Fork elk herd one of the most prolific in Montana, with a cow-calf ratio often exceeding 50 percent. Chalk-white limestone cliffs riddled with caves buttress the lower four miles of the Middle Fork as it leaves the mountains.

Sapphires glittered for early-day miners along the Middle Fork, but its real treasures are the unspoiled horizons that inspired Charlie Russell and that continue to capture our dreams.

The Smith and Musselshell rivers are separated by a ridge that forms the east boundary of the 8,800-acre North Fork Smith roadless area in the south-central Little Belts. Rolling parks give way to rounded limestone ridges that dip southward, dropping steeply into grassy-bottomed V-shaped canyons. Numerous elk calve in the north and then summer to the south near the Lewis and Clark National Forest boundary.

A prominent east-west ridge forms the 18-mile-long southern boundary of the 33,000-acre Mt. High roadless area on the east end of the Little Belts. From Mt. High sparsely timbered limestone canyons drop nearly 3,000' to the plains in this driest part of the range. Limber pine surrounds a balancing rock in Buffalo Canyon.

The highest point on a southeast Little Belts rock bluff is called Bluff Mountain, after which a 37,120-acre roadless area is named. Most of this wildland of narrow limestone canyons and high cliffs is so dry that only a few mule deer can make a living. The exception is the northwest corner, where large boggy meadows lie hidden in dense forests of lodgepole, spruce and fir. Fossils and prehistoric campsites await the inquisitive visitor. The country remains wild despite its penetration by 20 miles of primitive jeep trails.

Most of the 19,800-acre Spring Creek roadless area on the southern tip of the Little Belts is a thick carpet of lodgepole with parks scattered at all elevations. Deep solitude can be found in the narrows of lower drainages, which are like tunnels through the limestone. Tipi rings and ceremonial sites tell of long-ago travel by prehistoric Indians. Today, elk make year-round use of the country—from calving to winter foraging.

BILL CUNNINGHAM PHOTOS BOTH PAGES

Along the Smith River.

87

74 Big Snowies

The tilted limestone beds of the Big Snowy Mountains thrust 3,000' above a parched prairie sea just south of Montana's geographical center. From a distance, the east-west crest looks bare and flat above steep, heavily-timbered faces separating narrow avalanche chutes. Up close the summit ridge is indeed a flat tundra meadow for nearly half of a 22-mile-long expanse of wild country that occupies almost all of this high mountain island. The roadless perimeter of 104,755 acres includes the easternmost Montana Wilderness Study Act area as well as the Bureau of Land Management's contiguous and densely-forested 6,870-acre Twin Coulees Wilderness Study Area on the southeast corner of the range. The north side is moist enough to support lodgepole pine, spruce and Douglas fir. Bowl-shaped headwalls are carved into the dry craggy southern face of the arching Big Snowies.

Folding and warping of the sedimentary rock have given these mountains their distinctive personality—a broad, relatively flat crest with limestone cliffs, steep cirques and bowl-shaped canyons draining to the plains. On the east end, Knife Blade Ridge becomes easier to negotiate for mountain goats than for hikers; it follows a precipice that falls sharply on both sides. Views from the high point of the range—8,681' Greathouse Peak—encompass the entire width of Montana from Canada to Yellowstone. On the west end, spelunkers are lured to the Devil's Chute and Ice Cave as well as to several unexplored limestone caverns. The frozen-walled room of Ice Cave is typically 40 degrees cooler than the outside summer temperature.

75 Square Butte

Square Butte is best known as the backdrop in many of Charlie Russell's paintings. The real thing is even more impressive. The 5,684' butte, rising 2,400' above the prairie, is a laccolith or volcanic domed tower of flat-topped igneous rock surrounded by eroded spires. Dark-colored dikes radiate for miles across the plains. In striking contrast, the butte is crowned with white vertical cliffs.

A 1956 lightning-caused fire established a doghair thicket of small lodgepole pine on top of the butte. Guarded by cliff walls, the plateau has never been grazed by livestock. This gives researchers a perfect opportunity to compare the "relict" vegetation of Square Butte with similar areas used by livestock.

Mule deer, antelope and even wandering elk are seen below the rim, where jutting slabs of rock provide sweeping vantage points. The cliffs also give refuge to about 25 mountain goats, the result of transplanting several animals to the butte in the early 1970s. Golden eagles, great horned owls and prairie falcons are among the many birds living on Square Butte during most of the year. With their camps at the base, early peoples climbed the butte for vision quests. In recognition of these values, the Bureau of Land Management manages the 1,947 acres of Square Butte as a natural area.

76 Highwood Mountains

Square Butte is actually an isolated dome of the Highwood Mountains, which rise abruptly to the west. The exposed rock walls of an igneous dike connect the butte to the main range. Geologists believe that this tight cluster of a dozen 7,000' peaks blocked the advance of continental glaciers 30,000 years ago. The Highwoods contain 39,900 acres of roadless meadows, forest and talus slopes bisected by a low-standard road that fords Highwood Creek

CHERYL M. MILLEY

From Square Butte near Geraldine, looking northeast.

a half dozen times, slicing the undeveloped lands into a western third and eastern two thirds. Narrow coulees with aspen groves lead to spacious, gently sloping meadows ringed by mature lodgepole pine and Douglas fir that sprang up after a large turn-of-the-century fire. The land is uncommonly lush for central Montana, which partly explains why a sizeable herd of 800 elk flourish in this compact, rectangular montane island.

77 Sweetgrass Hills

The Sweetgrass Hills of north-central Montana nearly touch Alberta, and form the smallest, most isolated, and northernmost of the intrusive mountain islands. High peaks rise 3,000' above the prairie to elevations approaching 7,000' within three major buttes, each of which is an eroded remnant of a separate laccolith.

In 1806, Lewis and Clark spotted all three buttes and called them "Broken Mountains." To the Blackfeet the hills were "Sweet Pine," named for the surprising occurrence of subalpine fir near the cool, moist summits of East and West Butte. Because of a mistranslation, these mountains are known to us the Sweetgrass Hills. Grasslands occupy most of the slopes of the buttes, which give rise to intermittent spring-fed streams flowing through steep canyons. Shady north faces are matted with dark forests of lodgepole, Douglas fir, limber pine and gnarled subalpine fir.

Because the hills protruded above the Wisconsin ice sheet, they may have been refuges for arctic-alpine plant species during the apex of the glacial period. This living laboratory is enhanced by its isolated lack of contamination from other plant communities.

The Sweetgrass Hills were the last sanctuary of the plains buffalo. The buffalo and resident Plains Indians are gone, but the hills still are used continuously for traditional religious practices by Native American people. Indeed, the Devil's Chimney Cave on East Butte remains a significant cultural site, as are Mt. Brown and isolated ridges above Tootsie Creek, for members of the Rocky Boys Reservation. Gold exploration roads have impacted Tootsie Creek, but the rest of East Butte to the north is pristine.

Present-day wildlife includes a herd of 200 elk, large numbers of antelope and both species of deer. West, Middle and East buttes have a combined area of about 20,000 acres—relatively inaccessible and little traveled, mostly because of steep terrain and surrounding private ownership. Within the igneous cones of East and West buttes is an essentially wild 6,957-acre core of Bureau of Land Management land, which is being designated an Area of Critical Environmental Concern. With this protection, it is hoped that the hills will continue to replenish the water and spirits of the land and people below, providing a sense of place through centuries of change.

78 Bearpaw Mountains

The Bearpaws are an 80-mile-long expanse of rounded peaks, grassy buttes, and timbered ridges rising 1,000' to 3,000' above the Hi-Line prairie southeast of the Sweetgrass Hills. When viewed from a mound near Big Sandy, the configuration looks like a huge paw print. The range is perched on the crest of a broad, gently warped arch called the Bearpaw uplift.

The Bearpaws are almost entirely privately owned and are criss-crossed by roads and jeep trails used for mining, logging and recreation. Many of the old roads have reverted to trails and many of the trails have been erased by lack of use. Today, a half dozen undeveloped, essentially roadless tracts totaling at least 50,000 acres are spread across the southern end of the Rocky Boys Reservation and onto adjacent private land to the south and east.

The highest and most pronounced feature is 6,916' Bearpaw Baldy, a central axis rising 2,000' in only one mile. Baldy is a gigantic mound of shale with rocky slopes falling steeply to dense Douglas fir forests. An unsurpassed view of almost all of the island ranges is available from the broad summit. Offerings tied to trees on the north side of the peak attest to present-day practice of traditional religion by tribal members. Baldy and Pecora Ridge lead to forests that are unusually moist and thick for eastern Montana. The country northwest of Baldy is marked by Bowery and Bailey peaks—almost 1000' lower and more gently rounded and open. The upper reaches of Beaver, Clear, and Little Box Elder creeks are home to a cluster of major peaks in the 6,000' range, which display a mosaic of thick Douglas fir, aspen groves, open-growing ponderosa pine and rolling grasslands. Wildlife includes a thriving elk herd and the puzzling recurrence of an occasional black bear after a 100-year absence.

Interestingly, even though the Bearpaws lack any formal protection, their undeveloped character remains virtually unchanged since the homestead era.

Total Wildlands in Prairie Islands Region:
 1,249,214 acres
Amount of Designated Wilderness: 28,562 acres (2.3%)

BILL CUNNINGHAM

The head of White Pine Gulch in the Bearpaw Mountains.

WILDLANDS OF THE LOWER MISSOURI

LEFT: RICK GRAETZ; BELOW: CHARLES E. KAY;
RIGHT: BILL CUNNINGHAM

The Missouri River has cut a canyon 600 to 1,300 feet deep, forming breaks that extend for 297 twisting miles across north-central Montana. Sedimentary shales and sandstone overlapped older sedimentary formations like layers in a cake. Later, these horizontal layers of rock were sharply uplifted. Today's Missouri Breaks topography was created during the Pleistocene when the ice sheet melted. The Missouri was forced south of the Bearpaws, digging deeply into soft shales and sandstones. The result is countless steep bluffs and deep coulees characteristic of the severely eroded breaks. Gradually these coulees merge into rolling plains, often 10 miles or more from the main channel. This remote wild region is rich in history, cultural resources and wildlife, as well as being an outdoor museum of vertebrate and invertebrate fossils.

Above: *Burnt Lodge Wilderness Study Area.*
Left: *Prickly pear cactus.*
Far left: *On the wild Missouri River.*

91

WILDLANDS OF THE LOWER MISSOURI

†For identification purposes in this book only
*Areas with contiguous wildlands in Idaho
**Areas with contiguous wildlands in Wyoming

KEY
Agency Symbols
BLM—Bureau of Land Management
FS—Forest Service
FWS—Fish & Wildlife Service
MDFWP—Montana Dept. of Fish, Wildlife & Parks
NPS—National Park Service
P—Private
S—State
SEA—USDA Science & Education Administration
T—Tribal
TNC—The Nature Conservancy

Management Status Symbols
ACEC—BLM Area of Critical Environmental Concern
BLM WSA—Bureau of Land Management Wilderness Study Area
FPA—Forest Service Further Planning Area
ISA—Instant BLM Study Area
NP—National Park
NRA—National Recreation Area
NWR—National Wildlife Refuge
ONA—BLM Outstanding Natural Area
PP—Private Preserve
R-NW—Roadless-Nonwilderness
RWMA—Recreation & Wildlife Management Area
SP—State Park
TPA—Tribal Primitive Area
TR—Tribal Reserve
TW—Tribal Wilderness
W—Wilderness
WMA—State Wildlife Management Area
WSA—Congressional Wilderness Study Area (Forest Service)

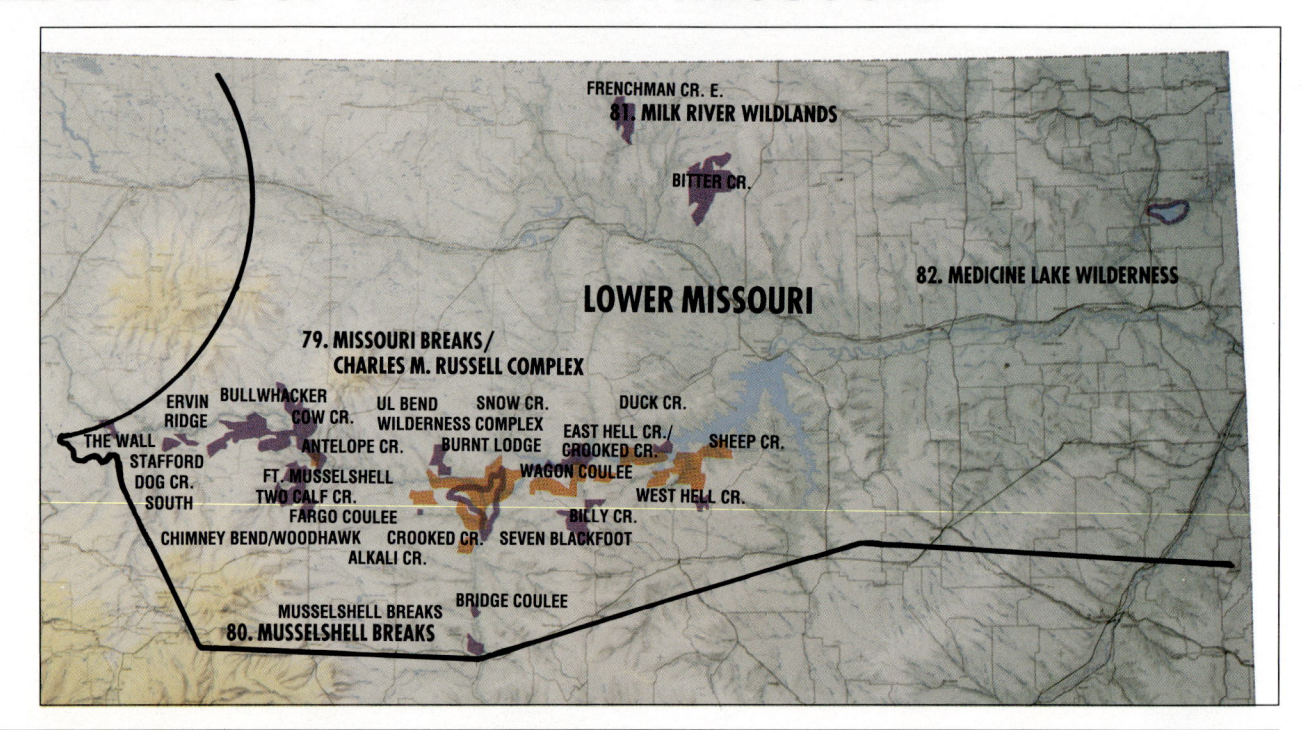

Physiographic region COMPLEX Area Name	Area No.†	Montana Gross Acreage	Agency/ Ownership	Management Status
VIII. Lower Missouri				
MISSOURI BREAKS/ CHARLES M. RUSSELL COMPLEX	79			
The Wall		12,200	BLM	R-NW
Dog Creek South		5,150	BLM	BLM WSA
Stafford		4,800	BLM	BLM WSA
Chimney Bend/Woodhawk		30,000	BLM	R-NW, BLM WSA
Ervin Ridge		12,880	BLM	R-NW, BLM WSA
Bullwhacker		10,000	BLM	R-NW
Cow Creek		50,000	BLM	R-NW, BLM WSA
Antelope Creek		17,900	BLM/FWS	R-NW, NWR, BLM WSA
Missouri Islands		917	BLM	R-NW
Two Calf Creek		9,220	BLM	R-NW
Fargo Coulee		5,000	BLM	R-NW
Ft. Musselshell		9,210	FWS/BLM	NWR, R-NW
UL Bend W & Contiguous		54,643	FWS/BLM	W, NWR, R-NW
Crooked Creek		14,340	FWS	NWR
Alkali Creek		7,990	FWS	NWR
Lost Creek		11,500	FWS	NWR
Burnt Lodge/Box Elder		42,930	FWS/BLM	NWR, R-NW, BLM WSA
Seven Blackfoot		50,400	FWS/BLM	NWR, R-NW, BLM WSA
Billy Creek		13,700	FWS/BLM	NWR, R-NW, BLM WSA
Wagon Coulee		11,088	FWS/BLM	NWR, R-NW
Snow Creek		6,760	FWS	NWR
Duck Creek		6,400	BLM	R-NW
West Hell Creek		13,480	FWS	NWR
East Hell Cr./Crooked Creek		22,514	FWS/BLM	NWR, R-NW
Sheep Creek		13,080	FWS	NWR
(Total Missouri Breaks Wildlands: 437,002 acres)				
(Total Contiguous Wildlands: 407,492 acres)				
MUSSELSHELL WILDLANDS	80			
Musselshell Breaks		8,650	BLM	BLM WSA
Bridge Coulee		5,900	BLM	BLM WSA
MILK RIVER WILDLANDS	81			
Bitter Creek		62,940	BLM	BLM WSA, R-NW
Frenchman Creek E		19,444	BLM	R-NW
MEDICINE LAKE WILDERNESS	82	11,366	FWS	W

Total Wildlands: 545,302 acres. Wilderness: 32,185 acres (5.9%)

79 Missouri Breaks/Charlie Russell Wildlands Complex

The last seven percent of the Wild Missouri is a National Wild and Scenic River for 149 miles, from historic Fort Benton downstream to the Fred Robinson Bridge just inside the Charles M. Russell National Wildlife Refuge. The Charlie Russell stretches for another 120 miles, enveloping Fort Peck Reservoir. From the Judith River country downriver, 25 roadless areas are managed by the Bureau of Land Management (BLM) and the U.S. Fish & Wildlife Service (FWS). They total 437,002 acres and border either the Wild Missouri, Fort Peck Reservoir or the refuge. Four of these wildlands, comprising 28,610 acres, are separated from the river by roads. The remaining complex of 407,492 acres is really one great 160-mile linear west-east wilderness from the Judith to the east end of the Charlie Russell. Although separated from each other by mostly low-standard roads that are impassable when wet, these 21 Missouri Breaks wildlands share the common thread of the Wild Missouri, making them in unison the fifth-largest roadless and undeveloped complex in Montana. One can stand on the cultivated benchlands above the Missouri and have no idea that the wild breaks are below. Conversely, when deep in the breaks, visitors have a profound feeling of being totally cut off from the world.

Mule deer are the most abundant large mammal in the breaks. Mature big-bodied breaks bucks display high sweeping racks, as opposed to the wider sets of antlers more common elsewhere. Whitetails are limited from Cow Island downstream, where brush adjoins crop lands near the river. Several transplants since 1951 have restored thriving populations of indigenous elk to densely forested portions of the breaks. The last of the Audubon bighorns were wiped out near Billy Creek in 1916. In 1979, 27 bighorn sheep were planted at Chimney Bend. The sheep have gradually expanded upstream as far as Stafford, and are readily visible from the river as they continue to repossess their historic range. Antelope occur sporadically but prefer the nearby rolling prairie. Sharp-tailed grouse thrive where grasses meet brushy coulees. Pheasants are found on islands and in river bottoms of impenetrable rosehips. The relatively warm waters of the Missouri are inhabited by sauger, catfish, walleye and paddlefish that often exceed 100 pounds.

Imagine that you are on an epic canoe trip down the Wild Missouri with time enough to explore each wild jewel in the necklace we call the Missouri Breaks, beaching on the north or south shore in the order in which each jewel presents itself—from The Wall on down to Sheep Creek.

The Wall is a narrow 12,200-acre band of undeveloped BLM land touching 15 miles of the north shore from distinctive Dark Butte to just above the Winifred Bridge. Cottonwoods parallel the river with the rugged, dissected face of The Wall appearing as almost solid prairie grasses and sagebrush. A closer look reveals tiny pockets of juniper and pine in sheltered coulees. Tipi rings on the bluffs overlook the remains of an old homestead.

Immediately downriver from the historic PN Ranch, BLM's 5,150-acre Dog Creek South Wilderness Study Area (WSA) occupies five miles of the Wild Missouri's south bank. Heavily-eroded open clay slopes drop almost vertically from narrow, barren ridges. Trees are few and far between.

The long, narrow 4,800-acre Stafford WSA stretches for nine miles directly across the river from Dog Creek. Flat ridges drop steeply at gradients often exceeding 90 percent with soils too loose to support vegetation. The more moderate slopes are covered with grasses, sagebrush and greasewood. The east boundary is an old wagon road once used to salvage a grounded steamboat.

Nearly 30 miles of the Wild Missouri serve as the northern boundary of the combined 30,000-acre Chimney Bend-Woodhawk wild area, only 8,100 acres of which is a BLM WSA on the east end. Although penetrated from the south by a dozen primitive ridgeline jeep trails, the rugged, deeply dissected terrain and its scattered but dense ponderosa pine and Douglas fir provide outstanding solitude. Colorful geological formations are matched by an equally colorful history. Woodhawkers cut timber to fuel steamboats; today their woodlots have regrown except in several large burns. The Woodhawk area likely was traversed by Chief Joseph's Nez Perce in their attempted 1877 escape to Canada.

On the north shore across from Chimney Bend, the 12,880-acre Ervin Ridge WSA heralds some of the more rugged badlands in the breaks. Differential erosion has created a jumbled array of mushroomed rocks, castles, monuments and arches along the river. Narrow bare ridges are flanked by steep clay sides with short prairie grasses and sagebrush. The more remote east end has scattered pockets of ponderosa and lodgepole

DENNIS HENRY

Mule deer buck.

Above: Ervin Ridge Wilderness Study Area, Missouri Breaks.
Right: Prairie rattlesnake.

pine, juniper and Douglas fir at the heads of protected draws.

Separated from Ervin Ridge by a low-standard road, the lower 10,000 acres of the Bullwhacker and Little Bullwhacker drainages are a wild continuation of the Missouri Breaks. The country is heavily dissected, with narrow coulees that feed into broad bottoms. More widely forested than most of the breaks, the terrain also supports diverse prairie grasses and ground-hugging forbs.

A wild 50,000-acre expanse surrounds the lower reaches of Cow Creek, most of which is within a WSA. Sandstone cliffs form walls above Bull Creek and Hay Coulee with the most spectacular wall being four miles of sheer sandstone on the west side of Winter Creek. Over time, water and wind have chiseled this face into castle-like formations. Prairie grasses, sagebrush and greasewood grow wherever the slope and soils permit. The north end displays dense stands of ponderosa and lodgepole pine, Douglas fir and juniper, with cottonwood groves along Cow Creek. The Nez Perce traversed the Cow Island Trail on the west boundary during their 1877 flight toward Canada. Much earlier people left tipi rings and a buffalo jump. A box canyon above Winter Creek, called "Horse Thief Pass," was used as a natural wild horse corral at the turn of the century.

The 17,900-acre Antelope Creek WSA is a series of highly eroded coulees dropping to the Refuge portion of the Wild Missouri. Steep slopes of exposed shale are separated by narrow finger ridges crowned with patchy Douglas fir and ponderosa pine. Much of the country is barren or sparsely vegetated with sagebrush and short prairie grasses. In the refuge portion of lower Antelope Creek, ponderosa pine and three species of juniper grow in the bottoms of long drainages. Kid Curry's outlaw hideaway is concealed on the northwest corner.

The west end of the Charles M. Russell National Wildlife Refuge is bordered by two BLM roadless areas totaling 14,220 acres. Two Calf Creek is a rough, broken land of heavy ponderosa pine and Douglas fir forest. In contrast, Fargo Coulee to the southeast is a more rolling landform of sagebrush prairie, sparsely timbered after repeated range fires.

The south shore of the refuge is bordered by the 9,210-acre Ft. Musselshell WSA, where the character of the Missouri changes from river to reservoir. Rolling terrain gives way to well timbered slopes interspersed with grasses and shrubs. In an unusual twist, drainages parallel the Missouri instead of running at right angles.

When the displaced Missouri River channel was carved along the southern face of the glaciers, it detoured widely around the "thumb" of ice that overlaid the pre-glacial valley of UL Bend. Today, the 20,819-acre UL Bend Wilderness is scattered among five unconnected blocks that border 33,824 acres of the Russell refuge and BLM wildlands around Mickey Butte and East and West Beauchamp. The peninsula of UL Bend is the most striking feature of this 54,643-acre north-shore wildland complex.

Lewis and Clark were the first white men to lay eyes on UL Bend. They camped at the mouth of the Musselshell on the opposite bank of the Missouri. Their journal entry of May 21, 1805 describes UL Bend: "In its course the Missouri makes a sudden and extensive bend toward the south…the neck of land thus formed, though itself high, is lower than the surrounding country and makes a waving valley…with a fertile soil which, though without wood, produces a fine turf of low grass, some herbs, and vast quantities of prickly pear."

It was springtime several years ago as I wandered across the gentle interior of UL Bend and thought about its colorful past. I could envision Blackfeet hunters stampeding bison over a sharp break near what is now the shore of Fort Peck Reservoir—a perfect buffalo jump. Whitened bones at the base of the embankment told the tale. My hike took me from rolling grasslands in the north into a large, virtually flat, T-shaped basin. Climbing at an imperceptible rise of four feet per mile, I reached the 2,700' high point in the Wilderness. Standing at the head of a narrow coulee I watched birds on the lakeshore 500' below. And what a variety of birds in this remote prairie—236 species identified thus far—with sharptailed and sage grouse, bald and golden eagles, prairie falcons and Swainson's hawks among the year-round residents. A slight stickiness in the soil left by a thunderstorm the night before reminded me of how, when wet, Missouri "gumbo" turns the entire country into wilderness—denying passage to even the most determined 4-wheel-drive enthusiast.

Across the reservoir from the west side of UL Bend rises a series of isolated breaklands in the refuge's 14,340-acre Crooked Creek WSA. Short, heavily forested drainages are interspersed with small grassy parks. The lengthy Crooked Creek drainage forms its southern boundary before veering south to become the eastern border of the 7,990-acre Alkali Creek WSA on its way to the Musselshell. Alkali Creek is similar to Crooked Creek with its dense pattern of short, timbered coulees.

A Russell refuge wildland of 11,500 acres in Lost Creek lies due south of Mickey Butte. Steep, open coulees on the west change to densely forested hills to the east. Small clearings in the timber conjure images of western Montana mountain parks.

The combined BLM/FWS Burnt Lodge WSA on the north shore encompasses 42,930 acres of the most rugged and spectacular country in the Missouri Breaks. Grasses and sagebrush on rolling Bearpaw shale hills and parks typify the area west of Killed Woman Creek. Steep badlands, gnarled peaks, and pockets of conifers are found in the east. Here severe erosion reveals sheer sandstone walls and castle turrets suitable for climbing. Most notable is a 75-foot-high sheer sandstone face extending more than 100 yards, above Wyatt Coulee, known locally as "The Wall."

Directly across the reservoir to the south unfold 50,400 acres in the Seven Blackfoot WSA managed by the FWS and BLM. A myriad of narrow shale ridges studded with ponderosa pine, Douglas fir and "gumbo sharksteeth" open up to vast, unconfined space punctuated with rugged breaks. The presence of Douglas fir this far east is uncommon and may be of scientific interest. Broad grassy swales surrounded by clumps of ponderosa pine in the south give way to more deeply eroded, sparsely-vegetated canyons in the north. A central basin is molded by erosion, leaving stark cliffs and rolling prairies, and exposing formations with fossilized dinosaurs, early mammals and marsupials.

Deep breaks continue to the immediate east in the 13,700-acre Billy Creek WSA; most of which is on the refuge. Exposed Hell Creek and Tullock formations have yielded the skeletons of dinosaurs and smaller reptiles. Short, steep-sided drainages are covered with grasses, sagebrush and greasewood, with fringes of timber. In the east,

BILL CUNNINGHAM

These hunters have set up camp in Woodhawk Wilderness Study Area—in the most rugged badlands of the Missouri Breaks.

95

rolling terrain with scattered trees has been made even more open by recent fires.

Flat, open prairie drops into rugged breaks on the reservoir's north side in the 11,088-acre Wagon Coulee WSA. Elk and deer are plentiful in the timbered benches and canyons of this refuge wildland.

The breaks become even more rugged to the immediate south in the refuge's 6,760-acre Snow Creek wildland. Patchy ponderosa pine adorns steep-walled canyons.

The isolated 6,400-acre Duck Creek roadless area is a dry tract of BLM land on the north boundary of the refuge. With almost no trees, its predominant shrub is juniper. Two deep, steep-walled canyons converge as they enter the refuge.

South of the reservoir, and on the refuge, the 13,480-acre West Hell Creek WSA is an unusual blend of breaks more typical of the Missouri west of the refuge and of badlands to the east. Pine trees exist, but most of this varied terrain is mantled with grasses and sagebrush.

The East Hell Creek WSA, along with BLM roadless lands to the south in Crooked Creek, comprise 22,514 acres of wild badlands with a jumble of carved and stratified buttes. Gumbo knobs, sandstone formations, multicolored sediment layers and dramatic cliffs combine with uninterrupted expanses to create a forbidding but spectacular landscape. Deep breaks with scattered ponderosa pine and juniper are the rule on the west, with open, rolling grasslands to the east.

The easternmost Missouri Breaks wildland is the 13,080-acre Sheep Creek WSA. Inconsistent and variable erosion patterns in the shale have made this stark, secluded place a true badlands. The dissected terrain is covered with grasses, some sagebrush, barren ground, and very few trees.

BILL CUNNINGHAM

Medicine Lake.

80 Musselshell Wildlands

South of the refuge two separate BLM WSA's border the east banks of the Musselshell River. With the river as its western boundary, the 8,650-acre Musselshell Breaks WSA rises from open bottomland to knife ridges in the north and to broad grassy benches in the south, where dense ponderosa pine grows at the heads of coulees. Spacious grasslands are thickly matted with prickly pear cactus. Slumping clay slopes contrast dramatically with rugged breaks and the flat, winding Musselshell Valley.

A few miles northward, the 5,900-acre Bridge Coulee WSA sends rugged drainages west to the Musselshell. The lower ends of the coulees are open grasslands with deep ravines and sage-covered benches. More remote upper reaches are rounded, light-faced with sandstone outcrops and studded with ponderosa pine. Unsurveyed segments of the Hell Creek and Tullock formations are exposed, and they have yielded excellent dinosaur skeletons only 50 miles northwest.

81 Milk River Wildlands

Up against the Canadian border, the glaciated Missouri Plateau of northeast Montana contains two Bureau of Land Management wildlands that drain into the Milk River. With sizeable Frenchman Creek as its western boundary, the 19,444-acre Frenchman Creek East country is divided roughly in half by a road. A number of deep, densely timbered coulees lead off from a large plateau on the east end. Prehistoric tipi rings and lithic scatters are widespread, and mule deer and sharptailed grouse are common.

To the southeast, and as long ago as 12,000 years, hunter-gatherers used what is today the Bitter Creek Wilderness Study Area, which encompasses 62,940 acres in three segments divided by roads. Flat to gently rolling terrain ranges from 2,500' in the south to 3,000' in the north. In places extensive erosion has formed barren badlands. Advanced erosion caused by a crack in the ice during late Pleistocene accounts for the "blowout" scenery of sand/shale "waves." Although classified ecologically as shortgrass prairie, Bitter Creek is probably closer to being a mixed grass prairie of wheatgrass, blue grama, native legumes, silver sage, creeping juniper, aspen and chokecherry. Renowned for magnum mule deer, Bitter Creek is also rarely visited by wandering elk from the Missouri Breaks and gray wolves from Canada.

82 Medicine Lake Wilderness

More than 10,000 years ago the prehistoric bed of the Missouri River wound through what is now Medicine Lake in the northeast corner of Montana. Then, like a giant plow, the glaciers smoothed out the land and pushed the course of the Missouri southward. As the glaciers retreated, buried ice melted in place to form Medicine Lake and the surrounding prairie potholes. Over time, the winds carried and molded sand from the shores of the lake into the dunes of nearby Sand Hills.

Today, the shallow 8,700-acre Medicine Lake and Sand Hills are an 11,366-acre designated Wilderness within a National Wildlife Refuge. Medicine Lake is the flattest and lowest of Montana's designated Wilderness areas. Only 90' separate the nadir from its apex of 2,025'. The distinctive rolling dunes of the Sand Hills are mantled with a blend of mixed prairie grasses, chokecherry and buffalo berry.

Each spring, some 3,500 white pelicans power their nine-foot wingspans to the islands of Medicine Lake to form one of the continent's largest nesting colonies of the huge, graceful birds. Only 30 miles from Canada, the Medicine Lake "port of entry" is a way station for hundreds of thousands of birds during spring and fall migrations—a dizzying display of more than 200 avian species. Perhaps the rarest migrant to Medicine Lake is the endangered whooping crane—a magnificent bird that can attain a height of five feet with a seven-and-a-half-foot wingspan.

By its nature this prairie-pothole Wilderness will never be overrun by recreationists. Still, it is necessary to close the lake to public use from mid-September to mid-November to protect staging waterfowl. The wildness of Medicine Lake exists in its own right as a haven for wildlife—an island of ecosystem health in a vast sea of intensive agriculture. This is a place where visitors can stroll quietly, listening to the lonesome call of the wild goose or perhaps, just maybe, to the far-away trumpeting of the whooping crane calling to our untamable past.

Total Amount of Wildlands in Lower Missouri Region: 5453402 acres
Total Amount of Designated Wilderness: 32,185 acres (2 areas) (5.9%)

Above: Hell Creek Recreation Area.
Left: Male greater prairie chicken.

WILDLANDS OF THE LOWER YELLOWSTONE

LEFT: DEL SIEGLE; BELOW: ED TYANICH;
RIGHT: WILLIAM MUÑOZ

The Yellowstone River resists the onslaught of change as it flows free for more than 400 miles across southeastern Montana. The lands it drains have not fared quite so well. Within this vast plains geography, only seven wildland areas or complexes—totaling about 378,000 acres—remain undeveloped. At this writing not one acre has received the enduring protection of Wilderness designation. In every instance, these wildlands are the rougher, more remote island-like mountains, terraces and breaks in predominantly public ownership. All the major Yellowstone tributaries join the river from the south and some, such as the Bighorn, Tongue and Powder rivers, harbor some of the wildest, least visited country in Montana.

Above: *Wild horses in the Pryor Mountains.*
Left: *In the Tongue River Breaks.*
Far left: *The Terry Badlands.*

99

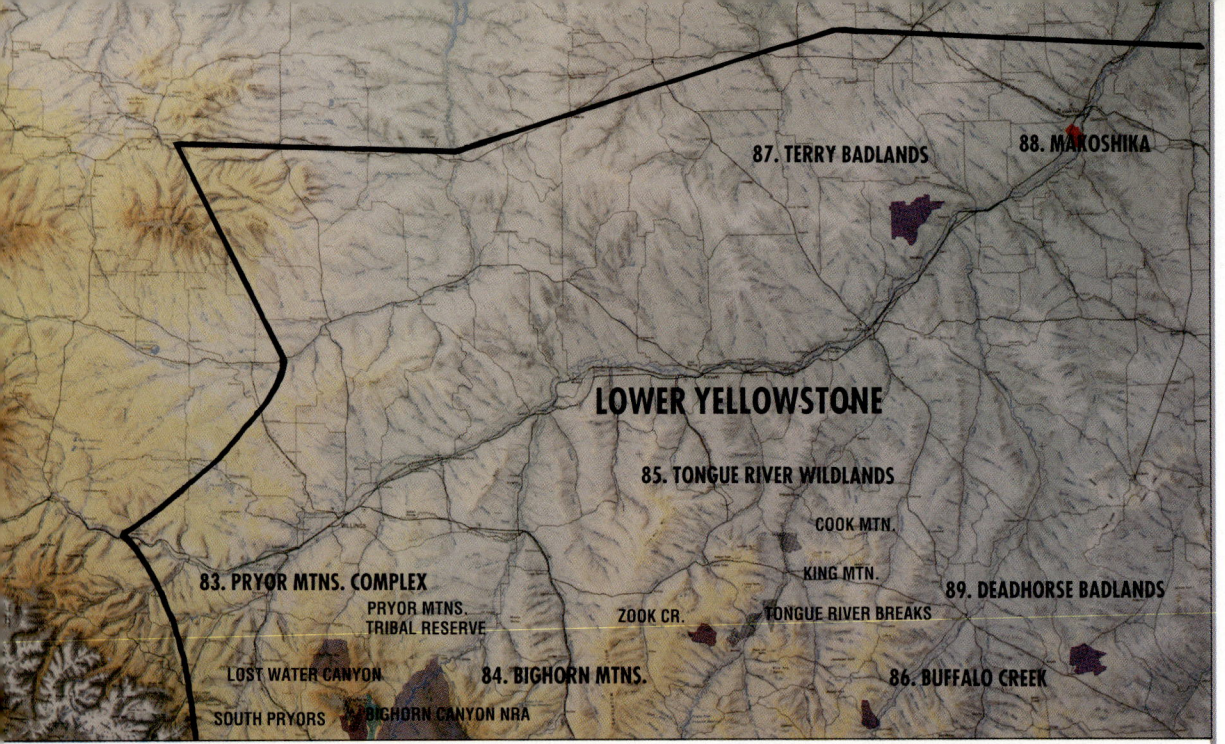

LOWER YELLOWSTONE

Physiographic region COMPLEX Area Name	Area No.†	Montana Gross Acreage	Agency/ Ownership	Management Status
IX. Lower Yellowstone				
PRYOR MOUNTAINS COMPLEX	83			
Pryor Mountains Tribal Reserve		45,000	T	TR
Lost Water Canyon		12,020	FS	R-NW
Bighorn Canyon NRA		17,000	NPS	NPS-NRA
South Pryors		21,000	BLM	BLM WSA
BIGHORN MOUNTAINS	84	150,000	T	TR
TONGUE RIVER WILDLANDS	85			
Cook Mountain		11,700	FS	R-NW
King Mountain		11,900	FS	R-NW
Tongue River Breaks		16,600	FS	R-NW
Zook Creek		9,078	BLM	BLM WSA, R-NW
BUFFALO CREEK	86	5,650	BLM	BLM WSA
TERRY BADLANDS	87	47,797	BLM,S,P	BLM WSA, R-NW
MAKOSHIKA	88	5,000	MDFWP	SP
DEADHORSE BADLANDS	89	25,890	BLM	R-NW

Total Wildlands: 378,635 acres. Wilderness: 0 acres.

†For identification purposes in this book only
*Areas with contiguous wildlands in Idaho
**Areas with contiguous wildlands in Wyoming

KEY
Agency Symbols
BLM—Bureau of Land Management
FS—Forest Service
FWS—Fish & Wildlife Service
MDFWP—Montana Dept. of Fish, Wildlife & Parks
NPS—National Park Service
P—Private
S—State
SEA—USDA Science & Education Administration
T—Tribal
TNC—The Nature Conservancy

Management Status Symbols
ACEC—BLM Area of Critical Environmental Concern
BLM WSA—Bureau of Land Management Wilderness Study Area
FPA—Forest Service Further Planning Area
ISA—Instant BLM Study Area
NP—National Park
NRA—National Recreation Area
NWR—National Wildlife Refuge
ONA—BLM Outstanding Natural Area
PP—Private Preserve
R-NW—Roadless-Nonwilderness
RWMA—Recreation & Wildlife Management Area
SP—State Park
TPA—Tribal Primitive Area
TR—Tribal Reserve
TW—Tribal Wilderness
W—Wilderness
WMA—State Wildlife Management Area
WSA—Congressional Wilderness Study Area (Forest Service)

83 Pryor Mountains Wildlands Complex

Mention the Pryors and images arise of thundering wild horses running free where the eastern edge of the Rockies meets the prairie. Indeed, our nation's first wild horse range encompasses 32,000 acres in the Pryor Mountains, which overlap much of a four-agency wildland complex of some 95,020 acres. About 45,000 acres within the remote northern terminus of the Pryors remain primitive and lightly visited. As a Crow Tribal Reserve, these wildlands are closed to non-members to safeguard cultural and religious sites. The complex also includes 17,000 acres of wild buttes, reefs and mesas within the Bighorn Canyon National Recreation Area on the east end of the Pryors. A central 21,000-acre core of three Bureau of Land Management Wilderness Study Areas includes the broken foothills and sonoran landforms of the wild horse range. Higher country, enveloping 12,020 acres within and around pristine Lost Water Canyon, is managed by the Forest Service on the northwest.

From semiarid deserts to subalpine mesas approaching 9,000', the area's topographic and vegetative diversity is unequalled. On the southern flanks, dry limestone canyons in high desert—such as Big Coulee and Burnt Timber Canyon—form an ecosystem not found elsewhere in Montana. Exposed marine fossil rocks display a dazzling rainbow of blues, greens, grays and Chugwater formation reds.

These mountains developed from vertical uplift, causing upfoldings of rock that often ruptured into faults on their northeast corners. The uplift, along with erosion, produced today's varied landforms of deep limestone canyons pocketed with caves, overhanging ledges, alcoves and canyon bottoms tough to negotiate because of dense underbrush and steep rocky talus. At higher elevations heavy forests of Douglas fir represent one of the easternmost extensions of the species. The Pryors also exhibit the most northerly growth of mountain mahogany.

Regardless of whether the wild horses are relict descendents of 17th century Spanish stock, as some believe, or are of more recent lineage, they coexist well with indigenous wildlife. Mule deer and black bears are plentiful in these almost inaccessible canyons and buttes, and smaller numbers of elk and bighorn sheep roam the land. Although most of the high desert streams are seasonal, short perennial stretches of Lost Water Canyon and Crooked Creek may harbor an isolated pure strain of cutthroat trout.

In spite of the inhospitable terrain, prehistoric peoples made extensive use of the country for camps, chert quarries, rock art, vision quests and migration. Ancient cave dwellers may have hunted mountain sheep here as long ago as 30,000 years.

84 Bighorn Mountains

The Bighorns are sacred mountains to the Crow Indians. Most of the range within the Crow Reservation remains wild because it is still used for traditional religious practice. As such, these tribal lands are closed to the public, thereby enhancing even more their resource of wildness. On a reservation where 30 percent of the land is owned by non-Indians, the northern and lower 20 miles of the Bighorns extending into Montana form the largest contiguous area owned by the tribe. The east side of Bighorn Canyon is bounded by sheer walls up to 1,000' high, with the Bighorn Canyon National Recreation Area reaching up to the rim. The canyon serves as the western and northern buttress of a wild expanse of at least 150,000 acres crossed by only a few jeep trails that wind over miles of open benches. Vast prairie plateaus with names like Devil's Playground and Dead Indian Hill tell of a colorful past. To the east stretches the expansive, sparsely-vegetated Garvin Basin, with elevations of 4,500' to 5,000'. The basin climbs 3,000' eastward up a series of perfectly formed open alluvial fans to steep, timbered ridges separating intermittent streams, topping out on 7,800' Big Bull Elk Ridge. Canyons and steep forested slopes in the north lead south to 1,200'-deep Black Canyon, where a dazzling array of multicolored formations rival those found within several national parks. Buffalo Pasture sits at the head of several densely-timbered northeast-flowing tributaries to Black Canyon. The Crow tribe keeps a herd of buffalo in the Bighorns, with a traditional annual harvest.

85 Tongue River Breaks Wildlands

The Tongue River Breaks is a maze of steep, severely eroded canyons that, collectively, contain four roadless areas totaling 49,278 acres. Three Custer National Forest wildlands drain to the Tongue from the east and one Bureau of Land Management Wilderness Study Area sits west of the river. Wind and water erosion constantly undercut sandstone walls, forming small caves and protected spaces that were used by Stone Age people for as many as 10,000 years. At the edge of an ancient plateau, the land plummets into V-shaped gullies that send water to the Tongue River after snowmelt and heavy summer thunderstorms. Tiny springs trickle from cracks in the rock but quickly disappear into the sandy soils of a near-desert prairie of juniper and sagebrush. Most of these wildlands are important mule deer summer habitat and each of the four areas contains winter range for deer, antelope, turkey and a few sharptail grouse.

On the north end of the plateau the gentle slopes of the 11,700-acre Cook Mountain roadless area descend north from 4,369' Cook Mountain. Steeper slopes with ponderosa pine define the Cook Mountain Divide, but most of the country displays gentle ridges with scattered pine trees gradually fading into open grasslands.

The 11,900-acre King Mountain roadless area is largely a series of west- or northwest-facing buttes supporting ponderosa pine and bunchgrass along a 4,100'-high divide. As the land drops to lower elevations along moderate, timbered ridges, the pine becomes scrubby, finally giving way to open prairie and juniper-sagebrush.

The 16,600-acre Tongue River Breaks area has remained roadless largely because of its rugged, deeply dissected terrain. These breaks and higher plateaus contain cultural sites of concern to the Northern Cheyenne. The vast flower-studded ponderosa pine parks of Poker Jim Flat provide a panorama of the breaks bordering both sides of the river valley. Folklore has it that when his boss caught him playing cards in the 1880s, Poker Jim left without a job but his name stuck to these rambling meadows.

Much of BLM's 9,078-acre Zook Creek Wilderness Study Area on the west side of the Tongue is covered by the reddish-pink of clinker—sandstone baked hard by burning coal seams. Chippings from early Indian tools can be found along the broken rock faces of formations, where bright red bands contrast with buff-colored sandstone. About two thirds of the wide-open Zook Creek drainage is dotted with ponderosa pine on a northern plateau that sends ephemeral streams in all directions. Zook Creek contains at least two sharptail grouse leks, or courting grounds.

86 Buffalo Creek

In 1876, the west bank of the Powder River just opposite the northwest corner of what is now the 5,650-acre Buffalo Creek Wilderness Study Area was the

RICHARD FERRIES

BILL CUNNINGHAM

Above: *Bighorn Canyon National Recreation Area.*
Inset: *Evening primrose grows in the Terry Badlands.*

101

site of the Reynolds Battle—a prelude to the Battle of the Little Bighorn. The country has changed little since then. Buffalo Creek is evenly divided by a north-south, 4,100'-high ridge that is heavily dissected by some of the most rugged breaks and canyons along the Powder River. The canyons drop more than 600' from rims of red clinker to lower reaches guarded by sandstone walls. Additional contrast exists between flat grassy ridges and green ponderosa pine on north slopes of a jumble of secluded side coulees. Abundant mule deer find refuge in these deep Powder River breaks, as do prairie falcons on cliffs overlooking Buffalo Creek.

87 Terry Badlands

Many of eastern Montana's wildlands are badlands and are thus self-protected by twisted tunnels of tortured topography in which soft sedimentary rocks are continuously eroded into strange, chaotic shapes: bridges, table tops, battlements, pinnacles, spires, scoria escarpments and haystack buttes. This is an apt description of Bureau of Land Management's Terry Badlands Wilderness Study Area, which encompasses 47,797 acres of contorted formations molded by thousands of years of wind and water action.

Terry Badlands is separated into an eastern third and western two thirds by the Calypso Trail. Emptying southeasterly into the Yellowstone River, deep parallel drainages are lined with colorful banded cliffs above rolling prairie grasslands dotted with scattered juniper. The more open southeast corner touches the Yellowstone at 2,180', rising to 2,900' on undulating benches, and then up to extremely rough badlands holding sunken gullies bounded by eroded side slopes. During spring, summer and fall the most abundant large residents are mule deer and grouse, along with a few wild turkeys. One of the most easterly stands of limber pine grows atop the rugged northern rims. Of perhaps some historic interest, U.S. Cavalry troops carved graffiti on Sheridan Butte in the Badlands during the 1870s.

88 Makoshika Badlands

Makoshika Badlands is actually a redundancy in that "maco sica" means "badlands" or "stinking earth" in the Sioux dialect. In 1864, General Sully described this eerie landscape vividly as "hell with the fires out." The 8,834-acre Makoshika State Park just south of Glendive contains about 5,000 acres of roadless wildland—a small area that seems an endless maze of broken hills, washed-out gullies, twisting coulees and hidden chasms. The clays, silts and sands of this ancient river bed were deposited in horizontal layers some 200 million years ago when streams carried their loads eastward from the forming Rocky Mountains. Much later, internal forces caused the surface to break and tilt. A good example of this is the Cedar Creek Anticline beneath Makoshika. Thin black bands of coal between layers of sandstone and shale remind us of a warmer tropical time of dense vegetation, brackish swamps and dinosaurs. The fossilized remains of these extinct giant reptiles have been uncovered in the Badlands, including mammal teeth, turtle shells, gar fish scales and a crocodile skull. Present wildlife include large migrations of dark, red-headed turkey vultures. Ancient and eerie, the "buzzards" symbolize the badlands as they soar for hours over bare, warm buttes and pine-covered ridges.

89 Deadhorse Badlands

Constant wind, fickle weather, no potable water and rattlesnakes make the Deadhorse Badlands of extreme southeast Montana less than inviting for recreation, except perhaps for hunting mule deer and the few antelope. "Don't get lost in there," the local rancher cautioned. "You might never be found." The dominant feature of this 25,890-acre expanse of undeveloped Bureau of Land Management low-lying badlands is Alzada Ridge, which runs east-west and about 200' above deeply eroded benches and coulees. The topography produced by smaller ridges that radiate off Alzada is gentle to the north and more broken in the south. Cottonwoods mark the bottom of the East Fork of TL Creek, which flows north through flat grasslands and sagebrush. A dozen small mesas and buttes dot the horizon along the northern boundary. The largest butte, flat-topped with near-vertical sides, is likely an ungrazed enclave within a sea of prairie sheep and cattle allotments.

Total Wildlands in Lower Yellowstone Region: 378,635 acres
Total Amount of Designated Wilderness: 0 acres

BILL CUNNINGHAM PHOTOS

Above: *Deadhorse Badlands.*
Top: *Makoshika.*

Facing page: *Daisies brighten a Badlands spring day.*

FOR FURTHER INFORMATION

Myriad local, state, regional, and national groups working on wildland conservation issues have offices, chapters, or affiliates in Montana. If you are interested in a particular locale or issue, one of these organizations can direct you to the right place.

The Montana Wilderness Association

The Montana Wilderness Association (MWA) is the oldest state-wide wilderness conservation group in the nation, born in Bozeman in 1958—a half dozen years before passage of the Wilderness Act. Popular programs of this active grass roots organization include summer Wilderness Walks into threatened wildlands, and an exciting annual convention during the first weekend of December. The Helena office features a professional staff with lots of advice on how you can become more involved. Members receive the special journal, *Wild Montana,* and a bimonthly newsletter, *Letter Be Wild.*

Montana Wilderness Association
P.O. Box 635
Helena, MT 59624
(406) 443-7350

Alliance for the Wild Rockies

The Alliance for the Wild Rockies (AWR) is establishing a bioregional network to protect as much as possible of the remaining wildlife, wildland and wild rivers of the Northern Rockies, including the roadless lands of Montana. Members receive *The Networker,* a quarterly digest of Northern Rockies wildland issues, plus timely alerts. Contact the AWR staff for a listing of local organizations.

Alliance for the Wild Rockies
P.O. Box 8731
Missoula, MT 59807
(406) 721-5420

MICHAEL CRUMMETT

EPILOGUE

Whether you skimmed through the photos or read every word, you've covered a lot of country since opening the first page of this book. Montana is aptly called the Treasure State, but its real treasure is not what lies buried in the ground. A string of wild pearls dot the northern Bitterroot Divide, gem-like tarns sparkle in Jewel Basin, the Sapphire Mountains hold fast to stillness and solitude. These hidden places—large and small, steep and gentle, high and low, lush and dry, known and unknown, close and remote—make Montana and those who live here rich beyond measure.

Allocation and management—those are bureaucratic buzz words for dividing up the wildland pie. Then, once it is divided, we must figure out how to care for those slices we call wilderness. Montana's major Wilderness battles have been waged and the last of the big allocation decisions are at hand. Wilderness brings out our strongest emotions, so while the larger battles may be ebbing, an occasional skirmish will keep the pot boiling as long as we have both emotions and wild country.

Few, if any, of those who oppose preservation do so because they want to destroy wilderness. Their motivation is for family, livelihood, lifestyle and community. This must be seen and respected by those who advocate protection of wildlands, for their motivations are equally sincere. Mutual respect can lead to real communication, which can lead to the kind of understanding needed to find common ground. At no time has this common ground been better shared than when Montana millworkers and conservationists hammered out the historic Kootenai and Lolo wilderness accords of spring 1990. The rancher's concern for the watershed, the logger interested in a sustainable timber industry, the mill worker who enjoys camping with his family in a favorite backyard roadless area, and the sportsman wondering if his kids will be able to stalk wild elk in wild country are all after the same thing: quality.

An epic two-week pack trip across the Bob Marshall Wilderness may be a once-in-a-lifetime experience. But getting to know and nurture that pocket of wildness closest to your home, no matter how small, can be much more frequent and satisfying. There you can make a stand, live a philosophy, become intimate with a place, pass something lasting on to your children, and find the common ground with others in your community who, in the final analysis, want what you want. Even if we avoid the "W-word" and call it something else.

Picture the first light of a new dawn beginning to filter across the open benches of Deadhorse Badlands in eastern Montana, spreading over a vast, uncluttered landscape, and eventually brightening the rocky summit of Northwest Peak with the promise of a more enduring co-existence between people and our last remaining wildlands.

A Centennial nighthawk.

MICHAEL CRUMMETT